Writing the Way

The Story of a Spiritual Classic

Writing the Way

The Story of a Spiritual Classic

by RUSSELL SHAW

Scepter

Copyright © 2010, Russell Shaw

The total or partial reproduction of this book is not permitted, nor its informatic treatment, or the transmission of any form or by any means, either electronic, mechanic, photocopy or other methods, without the prior written permission of the owners of the copyright.

Copyright © 2010, Scepter Publishers, Inc.
P.O. Box 211, New York, N.Y. 10018
www.scepterpublishers.org

Printed in the United States of America

ISBN-13: 978-1-59417-087-4

Contents

Chapter One Books of Fire   1

Chapter Two A Profitable Lesson for Our Soul   19

Chapter Three The Writing of *The Way*   39

Chapter Four Up the Inclined Plane   52

Chapter Five The Originality of St. Josemaría Escrivá   85

Acknowledgment and Sources   101

CHAPTER ONE

Books of Fire

"I know how little virtue and knowledge I have, but I would still like to write books of fire."

This is St. Josemaría Escrivá speaking. It's August 7, 1931, and the Spanish priest is twenty-nine years old. Three years earlier he'd founded Opus Dei, but hardly anybody has heard of it yet. As a matter of fact, hardly anybody has heard of Josemaría Escrivá yet. In time that will change.

Books of fire, he explains in his Intimate Notes, are books that can "race across the world like burning flames and set people ablaze with their light and heat, turning poor hearts into red-hot coals to be offered to Jesus as rubies for his royal crown." Here's a typically impassioned expression of St. Josemaría's supreme ambition: he wants to do something really great—for Christ and for the men and women with whom he yearns to share his fierce love of God.

When the time comes, though, he won't see *The Way*—the book that is to be his most popular and influential literary effort—as the sort of book to accomplish that. Its aims will be too modest, its origins too humble, to meet the standards of a book of fire. At best, he'll suppose when it's published in 1939, it may sell a few thousand copies.

Which is additional evidence that people who want to make God laugh need only tell him their plans.

Why This Book?

Why write a book about St. Josemaría's book? That's easy.

The Way is a small volume, often published in a pocket- and purse-sized format intended for people who don't have a lot of spare time and want to make good use of the time they have, even in circumstances—a bus or subway ride, a wait in an airport—that may not look very prayer-friendly. The book consists of 999 short "points"—a few sentences or a couple of paragraphs at most—which are meant to serve as starting points for meditation and personal prayer.

It's no surprise that the faithful of Opus Dei, the predominantly lay group St. Josemaría launched in 1928 to promote sanctity in everyday life, should cherish *The Way*. Yet the author made it clear that it wasn't written "only for us." Rather, he attempted to write it in such a way that it would speak to anyone with a serious interest in the interior life, even making changes in his preliminary notes with that aim in view. Apparently he succeeded. Although as of 2009, when this is being written, the members of the Work (or, to be more formal, the faithful of the Opus Dei prelature) number only about 87,000 worldwide, sales of *The Way* in the first seventy years since its publication exceeded 4.5 million and it has been translated into forty-three languages.

Since it first appeared, just after the Spanish civil war, the book has touched and changed the lives of countless readers and been hailed as a modern spiritual classic. For thousands of people today it's a well-loved companion and guide in their efforts to build up and sustain friendship with Christ. A book like that deserves a closer look—to learn how it came to be written and, to the extent possible when discussing the operation of grace, to find the explanation of its perennial appeal to so many persons of such diverse nationalities and backgrounds.

The Way also deserves our attention for another reason.

Many books lack personality. For all the flavor and individuality they have, they might have been written by literate robots. Bookstores and libraries are full of such books. But *The Way* has vitality, character, a distinctive voice. One might say of it what the historian Henri Daniel-Rops says of the letters of St. Paul: while the author has obvious literary skills, the real strength of his writing is that he's "not a writer first of all, but a man," whose words aren't "products of a mind securely sheltered in a library, but . . . of a conqueror, a fighter, whose whole life was risk."

St. Josemaría's voice can be heard in the author's preface to *The Way*, speaking to the reader in affectionate, intimate terms.

Read these counsels slowly.
Pause to meditate on these thoughts.
They are things that I whisper in your ear—
confiding them—
as a friend, as a brother, as a father.
And they are being heard by God.

I won't tell you anything new.
I will only stir your memory,
so that some thought will arise
and strike you;
and so you will better your life
and set out along ways of prayer and of love.

And in the end you will be
a more worthy soul.

These few lines sum up St. Josemaría's aims in writing. He writes as a friend: because he tells readers what he thinks they need to hear, with empathy but also with unflinching candor. He writes as a brother: because he is intensely conscious that he is a child of God—"divine filiation," he calls it—and urgently desires that others, too, be aware of themselves as God's children; and because, precisely as God's children, all of us are members of the same family, the family of God, and therefore, in Christ, sisters and brothers to one another. And he writes as a father: because above everything else he wants us to grow up, to mature in divine filiation, and become saints.

But, someone might ask, why that reference to "things that I whisper in your ear"? If what the author has to say is really so important, why doesn't he shout? The answer, I think, is that *The Way* embodies the principle of *cor ad cor loquitur*, heart speaking to heart, which John Henry Newman took for his motto as a cardinal. This intimate discourse—spiritual direction, to give it its usual name—doesn't occur by shouting; it's conducted with that moral refinement of which discretion, confidence, and respect for the other are essential features.

The Way, then, is a book brimming with something St. Josemaría understood, prized, and wrote about vividly: heart. "You're afraid of becoming distant and cold with everyone—you want so much to be detached! Get rid of that fear. If you belong to Christ—completely to Christ—he will give you fire, light and warmth for all men" (*The Way*, no. 154). To read St. Josemaría's book thoughtfully and prayerfully is to enter into conversation with the man who wrote it. But as he wished, it's also, and especially, to enter into conversation with Christ. And finally to give Christ your heart.

The Universal Call

The fundamental idea underlying *The Way* was revolutionary when it came out. In many respects, it's revolutionary even now. Although the idea has been part of the authoritative teaching of the Catholic Church at the highest level ever since the Second Vatican Council of 1962–1965, it remains far from being heeded and taken seriously by all Catholics.

The idea is that holiness is for everyone, including ordinary Christians who live in the secular world and there carry out their responsibilities as spouses and parents, workers and professional people, students, citizens, neighbors, friends, and members of the Church. This is the "universal call" to holiness.

In modern times, this idea of a universal call is, as a practical matter, new. For centuries it was commonly supposed that holiness was the business of priests and nuns. The rest were expected to perform their duties of state and to avoid serious sin; and in this way they could expect eventually to reach heaven. But sanctity, the holiness of saints, was beyond the reach of most laity.

Vatican Council II in its Constitution on the Church set aside this way of thinking. The council taught: "It is therefore quite clear that all Christians in any state or walk of life are called to the fullness of Christian life and to the perfection of love, and by this holiness a more human manner of life is fostered also in earthly society.... The forms and tasks of life are many but holiness is one.... All Christians, in the conditions, duties and circumstances of their life and through all these, will sanctify themselves more and more if they receive all things with faith from the hand of the heavenly Father and cooperate with the divine will, thus showing forth in that temporal service the love with which God has loved the world" (*Lumen Gentium*, 40, 41).

In no way does it subtract anything from the originality and the importance of this teaching of Vatican II to point out that at the time the council said it, Josemaría Escrivá had been saying the same thing for nearly four decades. It is the message of *The Way*: "You have the obligation to sanctify yourself. Yes, even you. Who thinks this is the exclusive concern of priests and religious? To everyone, without exception, our Lord said: 'Be perfect, as my heavenly Father is perfect'" (no. 291). In this view, lay people become holy precisely by their lives as normal people living in the secular world of which they are fully part.

That has a special—and embarrassing—relevance for me in light of something that happened many years ago but still makes me blush whenever I think of it.

Ill-prepared for the assignment though I was, I'd been invited to give a talk about lay spirituality at a Catholic seminary. Being young and ignorant of just how ignorant I really was, I thought I'd give it a try. I said that the conditions of life in the world—the pressures of work, the demands of family life, the temptations of sociability, self-seeking, and sensuality which are so plentiful in a secular environment—rule out anything that might reasonably be described as a lay spirituality. The most that might perhaps be attempted by someone with a hankering for transcendence, I informed my audience, was to escape now and then from life in the world—get away from job, family, social life, and all the rest—and hole up in a monastery or some similarly isolated setting in order to soak up a bit of monastic spirituality, rather like a sick man dropping by an emergency room for a quick blood transfusion or a pick-me-up shot of oxygen.

Now, occasional spiritual retreats, conducted in silence in surroundings apart from the customary hustle and bustle, are certainly useful opportunities to get more in touch with yourself and with God than you usually do. But the naïve version of the spiritual quest that I proposed was far removed from what Vatican II had in mind in calling on lay people to seek holiness "in the conditions, duties and circumstances of their life." Nor was it the message of St. Josemaría, who insisted that God had placed the laity in the world so that they would achieve sanctity there and, in the process, sanctify the world itself as their specifically *lay* apostolic task.

Note, though, that St. Josemaría had no patience with the suggestion that the laity should infiltrate secular institutions like a pious fifth column and work secretly from within so as to win over these institutions to the side of religion. "I hope the time will come," he said in a 1968 interview with a Vatican weekly, *L'Osservatore della Domenica*, "when the phrase 'the Catholics are penetrating all sectors of society' will go out of circulation because everyone will have realized that it is a clerical expression." Lay people, he insisted, didn't have to "penetrate" secular society because they already were *there* as a matter of right and duty. Precisely in their roles as citizens, workers, students, neighbors, husbands, wives, and parents like all the rest, they were called to infuse this world to which they already belonged with the values appropriate to believing Christians.

That was his position from start to finish. In 1966 he told an interviewer from *The New York Times*: "To love and serve God, there is no need to do anything strange or extraordinary. Christ bids all men without exception to be perfect as his heavenly Father is perfect. Sanctity, for the vast majority of men, implies sanctifying their work, sanctifying themselves in it, and sanctifying others through it. Thus they can encounter God in the course of their daily lives." *The Way* is a guidebook for people who want to do that.

It's also important to understand that, in the view of St. Josemaría as in the view of Vatican Council II, lay Catholics aren't second-class members of the Church.

John Henry Newman had made that point memorably a century earlier, when, in an interview with a bishop who was trying to ease him out of the editorship of a Catholic magazine, he laconically remarked of lay people that the Church "would look rather foolish without them." St. Josemaría not only held the same view but carried the thought further. In a seminal letter of 1932 addressed to members of Opus Dei, he dismissed as "prejudice" the idea—at that time common even in advanced ecclesiastical circles—that in carrying on the work of the Church the laity were merely "helping the clergy." On the contrary, he held, the apostolic mission of lay people is "fulfilled in their profession, their job, their family, and among their colleagues and friends."

More than thirty years later, citing that passage shortly after the council, he added: "Today, after the solemn teaching of Vatican II, it is unlikely that anyone in the Church would question the orthodoxy of this teaching. But how many people have really abandoned the narrow conception of the apostolate of the laity as a pastoral work *organized from the top down*? How many people have got beyond the previous 'monolithic' conception of the lay apostolate and understand that it can and indeed should exist without the necessity of rigid centralized structures, canonical missions, and hierarchical mandates?"

Pope John Paul II hammers home ideas like these in *Christifideles Laici*, a landmark 1988 document on the vocation and mission of the laity. "Because of their baptismal state and their specific vocation... the lay faithful participate in the priestly, prophetic and kingly mission of Christ," the Pope declares. Half a century earlier, a young Spanish priest preached the same message in *The Way*. If ever a book was ahead of its time, it was this one.

Critics and Admirers

Not everybody who reads *The Way* likes it. That's no surprise, since it would be hard to think of any book that everyone without exception does like. *The Way* has been called shallow and unimaginative, a manual for those who might dismissively be described as Boy Scouts and Girl Scouts of the spiritual life. Sometimes even good people report looking into the book and concluding that it isn't for them. "I find what it says either too obvious or too obscure," a friend of mine once told me. That's how it is with people and books. There are those who enjoy coffee and licorice, The Beatles and Wagner—and those who don't. Perhaps some of those good people who don't see much for them in *The Way* at this particular point in their lives will appreciate it later. Or perhaps they won't. They'll still be good people.

In the eyes of some critics, though, the problem with the book apparently resides in the fact that it lacks the existential angst of a writer like Kierkegaard, to say nothing of the bombastic nihilism of Nietzsche. Kierkegaardian anxiety and Nietzschean nihilism are indeed missing from *The Way* (for which some readers may give thanks), but St. Josemaría nevertheless provides an adequate account of the dark side of life in a passage like this: "After losing those human consolations you have been left with a feeling of loneliness, as if you were hanging by a thin thread over the emptiness of a black abyss. And your cries, your shouts for help, seem to go unheard by anybody."

Instead of leaving it at that, however, the author offers an antidote: "The truth is you deserve to be so forlorn. Be humble; don't seek yourself; don't seek your own satisfaction. Love the cross—to bear it is little—and our Lord will hear your prayer. And in time, calm will be restored to your senses. And your heart will heal, and you will have peace" (*The Way*, no. 726). That's to say: Stop feeling sorry for yourself, my friend, turn to God for help, and get on with your life. Connoisseurs of alienation may consider that too pedestrian for their tastes, but others will see it as sound advice in most ordinary cases of self-pity.

One man's experience of reading *The Way* for the first time and not liking it points to still another source of some negative reactions.

For some time he'd been hearing here and there about Opus Dei and a book called *The Way*. He had no clear notion of either, but he'd picked up the idea that the book was something special. One day (this was back in the mid-1960s) he came across a copy—in a drugstore, he thinks—and bought it out of curiosity. Now he'd find out for himself.

I've seen that copy of *The Way*. It's a small paperback with a black and white photo on the cover, shot looking down on a crowd of people milling outside what appears to be the entrance of a large church, most likely St. Patrick's Cathedral in New York. Above the title, *THE WAY*, printed in multicolored capital letters, is this: "A book of spiritual rules that has become a religious classic . . . It has been called 'the *Imitation of Christ* of modern times.'"

Spiritual rules? Hmm. . . . Surprising that this man didn't quit right then and there.

On the copyright page the publisher is identified as All Saints Press, "a division of Pocket Books, Inc." This edition is said to be published by arrangement with Scepter Press. It is dated February, 1963. No price is given, but back then a modest paperback like this probably would have sold for under a dollar. The pages of the copy I've seen have turned brown at the edges, but the binding is intact.

Proceeding to the text, you find an introduction carrying the name of Cardinal Samuel Stritch, who was at that time the Archbishop of Chicago. "We hope that very many will use this little book and find in its words and wisdom the perfect way to follow Christ," the Cardinal writes. Next comes a three-page "editorial note" giving an overview of the book and offering a piece of advice: "To profit from *The Way*—and even to understand it—the reader requires a minimum of Christian formation, of a life of piety and of apostolic experience, of sacrificed [*sic*] concern for souls."

The man I speak of would have been smart to take that word of caution to heart, but apparently it went over his head. Perhaps he imagined that he measured up to those minimal standards. Be that as it may, in several sittings he read *The Way* from cover to cover—and was not impressed. Christian formation in large quantities he'd certainly received, but as for a life of piety, apostolic experience, and "sacrificed concern for souls," he knew nothing of all that beyond what he'd observed in his teachers and priests and a few other people. When he finished Escrivá's book, his reaction was simply: "I don't see what the fuss is about."

Now, in telling this story, I don't suggest that reading *The Way* straight through at the start can't be helpful for some people. In *Uncommon Faith*, his account of Opus Dei's early days, John Coverdale quotes an industrial engineer, later a member of the Work, who did exactly that and was moved to write: "One day a friend of mine lent me a book entitled *The Way*. It was the first I'd heard of it. I quickly thumbed through it and realized that it was extremely interesting. I remember exactly how I returned home, ate a quick dinner, shut myself up in my room and read the whole book at one sitting, from the first point to point 999. I also remember resolving to follow up that hasty reading with a much slower one. I was indescribably enthused . . ."

Very likely that was because he met the criteria for a fruitful reading of the book that St. Josemaría specified. They're along the lines of the editorial note cited above. Writing in 1934 to his friend Msgr. Francisco Moran, vicar general of the diocese of Madrid, about a predecessor of *The Way* published that year under the title *Consideraciones Espirituales* (as we shall see, its contents eventually were incorporated into *The Way*), Father Josemaría remarked that it would be "only useful for certain souls who really *want* to have an interior life; and to excel in their professional work, because this is a serious obligation." Years later, in 1966, he elaborated on that in answer to a question from the French newspaper *Le Figaro* that referred to *The Way* as a "spiritual code":

> *The Way* a code? Not at all. I wrote a good part of that book in 1934, summarizing my priestly experience for the benefit of all the souls with whom I was in contact, whether they were in Opus Dei or not. I never suspected

that thirty years later it would be spread so widely—millions of copies, in so many languages. It is not a book solely for members of Opus Dei. It is for everyone, whether Christian or non-Christian. Among those who have translated it on their own initiative are Orthodox, Protestants, and non-Christians. *The Way* must be read with at least some supernatural spirit, interior life, and apostolic feeling.

About *This* Book

The book you're reading now has two purposes. The first purpose is to introduce new readers to *The Way*. Of course there's no substitute for reading it, but an introduction may be helpful to people who've only recently become acquainted with it and, attracted and somewhat intrigued but not entirely sure what it's all about, would like to know more than is immediately apparent.

The second purpose is to help people who already know and admire *The Way* to understand it better—to see it in an even fuller, richer light, as one might better understand and become even more fond of an old and dear friend upon learning something about his or her childhood and youth. It's part of friendship, after all, to be happy in learning more about someone you love.

The history of *The Way* is surprising in several respects. The circumstances in which it was written hardly match the conditions of calm and recollection in which a book of spiritual counsel and prayer might be expected to take shape. (Very likely, its author would have been glad of more calm and recollection, but this looks suspiciously like another place where God had other plans.)

There was, for one thing, Father Josemaría's own unsettled situation—a young priest from the provinces, without resources, position, or reputation, but with a burning conviction that God had called him—of all people!—to launch a new group with a revolutionary message capable of shaking up the Church and changing the world, and to do this in the unpromising setting of a society torn by ideological conflicts and hurtling toward war. Much of *The Way* mirrors St. Josemaría's interior struggle to persevere in what, even to him, may often have looked like an impossible assignment—or anyway would have looked like one except for his deep faith that this truly was the Work of God.

In part, the book mirrors Spain in the 1930s—at the start of the decade, a fractured nation tormented by political impotence, mutual hatreds among classes and groups, virulent anticlericalism, and revenge-driven acts of violence; and from 1936 to 1939 torn apart by a bloody, brutal civil war. Along with providing an unintended spiritual profile of its author, *The Way* is filled with brief but memorable snapshots of scores of persons—university students, soldiers at war, bishops and priests, people deeply devout and deeply cynical with whom St. Josemaría came in contact in these tense and difficult years.

To some extent, too, *The Way* mirrors events on the larger stage of world history. What was happening in Spain was a kind of prologue to World War II and all that would follow, even up to the present day. A journalist who was Berlin correspondent for the *Manchester Guardian* sketched the ominous backdrop for the writing of the book like this: "We have referred to Marxism and National Socialism as secular religions. They are not opposites, but are fundamentally akin, in a religious as well as a secular sense. Both are messianic and socialistic. Both reject the Christian knowledge that all are under sin and both see in good and evil principles of class or race. Both are despotic in their methods and their mentality. Both have enthroned the modern Caesar, collective man, the implacable enemy of the individual soul. Both would render unto this Caesar the things which are God's. Both would make man master of his own destiny, establish the Kingdom of Heaven in this world. Neither will hear of any Kingdom that is not of this world."

The Way isn't about European politics in the 1930s of course, but its author was fully aware of what was happening in that larger world. His determination to stay out of political arguments kept him from discussing it at any length in his writing; but even so hints of the turmoil and tumult of those times bubble to the surface of the book. *The Way* was composed in the midst of continuing stress, anxiety, and—from mid-1936 until the end of 1937—in the face of real physical danger, for the author and his closest friends. Yet, for all that, it breathes a spirit of serenity, of trust in God, of love.

The sources of *The Way* have been examined exhaustively in a massive critical-historical edition, *Camino*, edited by Pedro Rodriguez and published in Madrid by Ediciones Rialp in 2002. The intention of the present book isn't to duplicate that monumental work, which will be an indispensable resource for scholars of St. Josemaría's thought for years to come. Rather, drawing on Rodriguez and others, the aim here is to touch on certain highlights of *The Way* that shed light on its meaning, while supplying a sketch of the biographical and historical background and, in the final chapter, a few thoughts on the originality of St. Josemaría and his achievement as a precursor of the new understanding of the role of lay people in the life and mission of the Catholic Church that was to be promulgated by the Second Vatican Council.

In its own modest way, this volume shares the intention of *The Way* itself: in the words of Bishop Javier Echevarria, Prelate of Opus Dei and second successor of St. Josemaría, "To inspire others to seek Christ and to help them find him"—specifically, with the assistance provided by St. Josemaría and his remarkable book.

A Guinness Stout of the Interior Life

In his carefully researched and reported study *Opus Dei*, journalist John L. Allen, Jr., remarks that the spirit of Opus Dei is to the spiritual life what that dark, strongly flavored beverage Guinness Stout is to beer. "In this era of new ecclesiastical brews," he writes, "Opus Dei offers a robustly classical alternative." To that one might add: Classical, yes; old-fashioned, no. From a historical point of view, as Allen points out, Opus Dei's "vision of laity and priests, women and men, sharing the same vocation and being part of the same body, all free to pursue that vocation within their professional sphere as they see fit, was so innovative that St. Josemaría was accused of heresy in 1940s Spain."

The accusations of heresy have died down by now, not least because Vatican Council II validated so many of St. Josemaría's insights. Yet in many respects Opus Dei and what it stands for remain something new and largely untried in Catholic life. Allen writes: "At its core, the message of Opus Dei is that the redemption of the world will come in large part through laywomen and men sanctifying their daily work, transforming secularity from within. 'Spirituality' and 'prayer,' according to this way of seeing things, are not things reserved primarily for church, a set of pious practices marked off from the rest of life; the real focus of the spiritual life is one's ordinary work and relationships, the stuff of daily living that, seen from the point of view of eternity, takes on transcendent significance. It is an explosive concept, with the potential for unleashing creative Christian energy in many areas of endeavor."

This explosive concept—standing alongside a "robustly classical" understanding of faith and the interior life—is present throughout *The Way*. Not surprisingly, some people even today find the combination hard to grasp. St. Josemaría expected as much. *"Nonne hic est fabris filius? Nonne hic est faber, filius Mariae?*—'Is not this the carpenter's son? Is not this the carpenter, the son of Mary?' This, said of Jesus, may very well be said of you, with a bit of amazement and a bit of mockery, when you *really* decide to carry out the will of God. . . . Say nothing, and let your works confirm your mission" (*The Way*, no. 491).

So what is *The Way* about? Something St. Josemaría said in a letter dated in 1940 to the faithful of Opus Dei provides a partial answer: "United with Christ through prayer and mortification in our daily work, in the thousand human circumstances of our simple life as ordinary Christians, we will work the miracle of placing all things at the feet of the Lord lifted up on the cross, on which he has allowed himself to be nailed because he so loves the world and us human beings."

That is what *The Way* is about. As you've probably guessed, I was the man who read the book many years ago and couldn't see the point of it. It's taken a while, but maybe I'm starting to get it.

CHAPTER TWO

A PROFITABLE LESSON FOR OUR SOUL

In later years St. Josemaría rarely spoke about what happened on October 2, 1928, and when he did, it was usually in a guarded manner. In this way he was practicing the "discretion" that he preached to others. For the momentous event which occurred that day, he explained, was "too intimately connected with the history of my soul" for him to share it casually with curiosity-seekers. Only now and then, for the benefit of Opus Dei members, did he provide a somewhat sketchy account. It went like this.

He and five other priests were making a retreat at the Vincentian Fathers' house in the Chamberi district of Madrid. The Vincentian house was located near the Foundation for the Sick, an institution conducted by a group called the Damas Apostolicas where St. Josemaría was chaplain. On the morning of October 2, the date in the liturgical calendar when the Church honors the Guardian Angels, Father Josemaría celebrated Mass, then went to his room before the retreat exercises resumed, intending to study some notes he'd brought with him.

He'd done the same thing often before. These handwritten notes were a private record of the hints and intimations he'd been receiving for years about something unknown to him, yet evidently specific, that he felt God wanted him to do. This feeling—that God wanted something out of the ordinary from him—had dogged him since his teenage years, and it was his sense that he could best respond to this calling, whatever it was, by becoming a priest that had led him to the seminary, to ordination, and now to this retreat. ("The priestly vocation!" he once exclaimed. "If [God] hadn't called me, where would I be now? I would probably be a conceited lawyer, an arrogant writer, or an architect enamored of my buildings.")

But here he was—a priest. In fact, a priest with a persistent sense that God was asking something more of him. But *what*? After all these years, he still didn't know. Often he prayed: *Domine, ut videam,* "Lord, that I may see," and *Domine, ut sit,* "Lord, that it may be." He may well have been praying those prayers that morning as he riffled through his notes.

Then it happened. He "saw" Opus Dei. "I received an illumination *about the entire Work*, while I was reading those papers. Deeply moved, I knelt down—I was alone in my room, at a time between one talk and the next—and gave thanks to our Lord." As he knelt, bells in the tower of the nearby Church of Our Lady of the Angels started to ring.

He didn't receive a blueprint for Opus Dei. Much was to come later, including the name. But what he had received was more than enough for the moment: a compelling vision of the vocation shared by all Christians to reach sanctity in and through the circumstances of their ordinary lives, and most naturally lived in the midst of the secular world doing ordinary secular work; an intense awareness that this heavenward impulse rising up from people living and working in the heart of the world was intended to become and to remain a powerful tool of God's redemptive action in history; and the humbling realization that he—yes, he!—was to be the human means through whom God would initiate this great work.

That knowledge, together with a sudden sense of God's special presence, made him fearful. But then the words "Do not be afraid" welled up in his consciousness. In the Old and New Testaments God and his messengers often speak these same words to chosen souls to whom God wishes to communicate a message. Not, St. Josemaría later wrote, that they—or he—sought a special sign of God's "extraordinary providence" or felt any less unworthy upon receiving it. But that "Do not be afraid" spoken in the depths of the soul nonetheless confers "an indestructible security, sparks in them impulses of faithfulness and dedication, gives them clear ideas about how to fulfill his most lovable will, and inflames them to hasten toward goals beyond merely human reach."

So it was for him. "On that day the Lord founded his Work," he said. "He started Opus Dei." He made it a point always to emphasize that this was God's work, not his. As for himself, at that time in October of 1928 his assets consisted of "twenty-six years, the grace of God, and good humor."

A Young Man without Resources

Looking back, you'd have to agree that there was not a great deal about this young priest visibly qualifying him for the task he now knew God had given him. To be sure, he was intelligent, devout, and eager to do God's will; but he was also almost entirely lacking in material resources, ecclesiastical and social connections, and the personal background that might have been thought indispensable for doing the job. For him, that pointed to an obvious conclusion: If God really wanted this new thing, God would have to stay closely involved in bringing it about.

Josemaría Escrivá was born in Barbastro, Spain, a little south of the foothills of the Pyrenees, on January 9, 1902. A visitor describes it as a place of "pleasant tortuous streets, old stone bridges, wine shops with great oozy barrels as tall as a man, and intriguing semi-subterranean shops." Running through the town was a "shallow jade-green" river overlooked by a perpendicular hundred-foot cliff pockmarked with doves' nests and houses built into the face of the rock. Altogether, a delightfully picturesque place for growing up.

The boy was the second of six children of Jose and Dolores Escrivá and the older of two sons. His father was partner in a shop that sold fabrics and made chocolates (a not uncommon dual arrangement in Spanish business establishments at the time). The family was close, loving, and fairly well-off. But sorrow entered the Escrivás' lives with the deaths in quick succession of three of the young girls. At the age of two, Josemaría himself contracted a serious infection and was not expected to live. But he did. In gratitude, his mother took him to the shrine of the Virgin Mary at nearby Torreciudad.

In 1914 family fortunes suffered a sharp turn for the worse with the bankruptcy of his father's business, resulting, it appears, from a general economic slump in the region along with costs incurred in a dispute with a former partner. Ignoring the advice of people who insisted he had no further moral or legal obligation, Don Jose Escrivá decided that the honorable thing to do was to liquidate his remaining assets and pay off his creditors. With that done, the family was left in serious straits.

After much searching, Don Jose finally found work as a clerk in a fabric shop in Logroño, a town of about 25,000.

His family joined him there in the fall of 1915, when young Josemaría was thirteen. Later he said he thanked God for this difficult period "because in that way I learned what poverty is." In these years, too, he began to have the feeling that he was being called by God. "I did not know what God wanted of me, but clearly he had chosen me for something specific. Whatever it was would come about in due course." Believing, as we've seen, that this calling involved the priesthood, he entered the seminary in Logroño in 1918 and two years later transferred to the seminary in Saragossa, a provincial capital with a population of 150,000, so as to study simultaneously at the law school there.

The young man was a good student, and his seminary years were successful. Still, there are hints that relations with his classmates—many of them farm boys lacking his genteel upbringing and pious habits—were sometimes strained. Someone hung the nickname "Mystical Rose" on young Escrivá, and on one occasion another student insulted him and the two of them traded blows. Mystical Rose he may have been, but he had a passionate nature and a quick temper.

In fact, he may well have had himself in mind when, years later, he wrote: "Why lose your temper if by losing it you offend God, you trouble your neighbor, you give yourself a bad time . . . and in the end you have to set things aright anyway?" (*The Way*, no. 8). One day his canon law professor told the class the story of a miller who made his own mill stones by letting rough rocks rub themselves smooth against one another in the mill. "That's how God treats those whom he loves," the professor concluded. "Do you understand me, Escrivá?" Evidently he did. "Friction produced by contact with others," he was to write, is needed to produce "the smooth and regular finish, the firm flexibility of charity" required in a saint (*The Way*, no. 20).

On March 28, 1925, not long after his father's death, St. Josemaría was ordained a priest. For the next two years he held temporary pastoral assignments in and around Saragossa and continued his studies in the law school, where he received a degree in 1927. Seeing no future for himself in Saragossa, he sought and received permission to move to Madrid in order to study for a doctorate in law. He arrived there on Easter Tuesday, April 19, 1927, and soon began abundant pastoral work as chaplain to the Damas Apostolicas and their Foundation for the Sick. In November he rented a small apartment for himself, his mother, his sister, and his younger brother.

Now he was a busy man, studying for the doctorate, doing pastoral work at the Foundation for the Sick and among poor people in outlying districts of Madrid with whom the Damas Apostolicas were in contact, while also teaching in a private academy and tutoring to make ends meet. And all the time the old question nagged at him: What does God want me to do?

He got his answer on October 2, 1928.

A Nation at Odds with Itself

To understand fully the challenge St. Josemaría faced after God's intentions became clear to him, it's necessary to know something about the situation in Spain and in the Spanish Church in those days. Putting into action what God asked of him with no visible resources would have been difficult in any circumstances, but at that time and in that place someone less confident than St. Josemaría that this was what God wanted might have been pardoned for considering the task well-nigh impossible.

By the early decades of the twentieth century, Spain's golden age was a distant memory. The farflung colonial empire was gone. The nation was politically, socially, and economically at odds with itself. For the previous century and a half or more, Spain had been torn by seemingly irreconcilable social tensions accompanied by occasional outbreaks of violence. Here was a country in a gradually escalating crisis and, for those with eyes to see, on its way to something worse.

For a long time, too, the influence of the Catholic Church had been in decline. Beginning in the eighteenth century, the antireligious propaganda of the Enlightenment worked to undermine Catholicism. In 1837 the Church's extensive land holdings were expropriated at the instigation of liberals and sold to middle-class speculators. In the face of attacks, the Church grew increasingly conservative and became ever more strongly linked with the established social order. Even so, historian Hugh Thomas describes the Church in Spain in the decades before the civil war as "charitable, evangelical, [and] educational"—that is to say, a benevolent and beneficent presence, albeit a somewhat old-fashioned one, on an increasingly troubled social scene.

By the turn of the century, however, the Church had become a kind of whipping-boy for hostile groups and interests—"a matter of obsession," Thomas says, to an assortment of enemies who included liberal politicians, Freemasons (often enough, themselves liberal politicians), resentful workers who'd been taught to blame the clergy for their troubles, and secularized, anticlerical intellectuals whose hostile fixation on the Catholic Church was such that they "could not forget the priests, even if they rejected religion." High up on the list of priorities for these forces was to drive the religious orders—commonly held to be "responsible for every cataclysm"—out of education; and this in a country that already had too few schools. (In Madrid alone, 80,000 children did not attend school in 1930.) Nor was the expression of this anticlerical mania merely verbal and political. In a notorious incident in 1923, for example, anarchists assassinated the Archbishop of Saragossa.

On paper of course the Spanish Church appeared overwhelmingly powerful. Nearly everyone was a baptized Catholic. In the 1930s there were some 60,000 women religious, 35,000 diocesan priests, and 20,000 male religious, together with a thousand monasteries and four thousand convents. Yet in this land that boasted a glorious Catholic history and countless monuments to faith, two-thirds of the people didn't practice their religion, except perhaps for baptisms, weddings, and funerals. In 1931 five percent of the rural inhabitants of New Castile made their Easter duty. In Andalusia one percent of the men in some villages attended Mass. Nor was this state of affairs limited to the countryside. In one well-to-do Madrid suburb, 90 percent of the graduates of Catholic schools did not go to church.

The year 1931 was a watershed. In local elections in April supporters of a republic won a majority of the votes. King Alfonso XIII, a stabilizing presence up to then, left the country, and the Republic was proclaimed. One of the first acts of the new provisional government was a declaration of religious freedom and separation of church and state. Early May brought the start of a campaign of anti-monarchist, anti-religious violence marked by attacks on a hundred churches and other religious establishments in Madrid and elsewhere.

Order was finally restored, but the government's slowness in intervening left a bad taste in many mouths. Tension, mutual suspicion, and the constant threat of violence had now become fixtures of national life. And the situation wasn't helped when the authorities—not without provocation, it must be said—expelled the Cardinal-Archbishop of Toledo and the Bishop of Vitoria for making anti-Republican statements.

By the autumn of the year the government had produced the draft of a new constitution whose religion clauses were, in Hugh Thomas's words, "ambitious but foolish." Among the provisions: government payments to priests, begun a century earlier as compensation for the seizure of Church lands, were to end in two years; religious orders were required to register with the justice ministry and would be dissolved if they were determined to be threats to the state; orders that required their members to take more than the three ordinary religious vows of poverty, chastity, and obedience—in other words, the Jesuits, whose senior members took a fourth vow of loyalty to the pope—would be dissolved in any event; religious education as such was to cease; any "public manifestation of religion"—a religious procession, for instance—would need government approval; and only civil marriage would be recognized as legal.

By now the scapegoating of the Catholic Church for the country's ills had become institutionalized, with the government in effect declaring itself officially anticlerical. For a long time reform elements had sought to bring Spain into the twentieth century, but now it was clear that the preferred means for bringing that about was to be the rigorous suppression of the Spanish Church.

Random anti-religious acts now became even more frequent. In Andalusia a priest who celebrated Mass under the open sky after his church roof was destroyed by lightning was fined for a public display of religion. Another priest was fined for being a monarchist after speaking of God's kingship on the feast of Christ the King. The ringing of church bells was taxed in one place. Elsewhere churches were burglarized and sometimes burned, without any serious effort being made to find and punish those responsible.

Not surprisingly, a reaction now set in on the part of what Thomas calls "Old Spain"—monarchists, the aristocracy, moneyed people, the middle-class, elements of the army, and many in the Church. The conservative political parties mobilized and started winning elections and parliamentary votes. As they did, their foes on the left became increasingly radicalized and determined to fight back.

The story of Spain in the years leading up to the civil war makes tangled and depressing reading. Anarchists, socialists, radicals, friends of the monarchy, communists, Catholics, Freemasons, the militant right-wing Falange, the army, the civil guards, parties, factions, and personalities of every imaginable ideological and political coloration, all constantly entering into coalitions of expediency that rapidly splintered, declaiming the rhetoric of idealism and social reform while bent on settling scores and quick to resort to violence—all had become locked in a vortex of incomprehension and mutual mistrust rushing toward an uncertain future. Perhaps the only thing even slightly clear was that whatever lay ahead was likely to be worse.

"Growing on the Inside"

And in this setting the young priest from the provinces, Josemaría Escrivá, set out to create a new force for the promotion of sanctity. From any reasonable point of view, he could hardly have picked a worse time. In the anticlerical atmosphere of those days, it could be dangerous for a priest simply to be seen on the street, and St. Josemaría, like other clerics, sometimes was the target of "insults and jeers." Yet his confidence was unshaken. "Your Work, Lord, will open their eyes!" he wrote in his Intimate Notes.

As we've seen, with the unraveling of the social and political situation in the spring of 1931, violence broke out in Madrid, Seville, and several other cities. For twenty-four hours, Father Josemaría recorded on April 20, Madrid was "one huge madhouse."

"Things seem to have calmed down," he added. "But the Masons do not sleep."

May 10 brought a fresh round of attacks lasting three days on churches, monasteries, and convents. Fearing for the safety of the Blessed Sacrament in the church of the Foundation for the Sick, St. Josemaría donned lay clothes and, accompanied by his younger brother, Santiago, wrapped a ciborium full of Hosts in a cassock and newspaper and carried it to the home of a friendly colonel.

Now and throughout his life, the priest made it a point to avoid talking politics. Nevertheless, as conditions deteriorated, he understood perfectly well what was happening and interpreted it in spiritual terms which he related to Opus Dei. Theologian Jose Luis Illanes writes: "The fact that a new historical scenario was emerging, often bringing with it a cultural crisis, was something quite easy to see at that time, as was also the need to foster among Christians . . . an attitude of faith which was both open and active, and which would encourage them to imbue their activities and thereby human institutions with the spirit of Christ."

Six years later, forced to take refuge along with friends in the Honduran consulate for fear of being shot or lynched by militias then roaming the streets, and with Spain already a battleground and the European continent lurching toward war, St. Josemaría was to speak of what was happening as the outcome of widespread failure of faith.

A point in *The Way* sums it up: "I'll tell you a secret, an open secret: these world crises are crises of saints. God wants a handful of men 'of his own' in every human activity. Then... *pax Christi in regno Christi*—'the peace of Christ in the kingdom of Christ'" (no. 301).

Still, there must have been times when even St. Josemaría was tempted to suspect that was easier said than done. Not only was the social situation threatening, but even the conventional mindset among people in the Church was inhospitable—to say the least—to unfamiliar talk about sanctity for lay people and a baptismal call to apostolate that came to the laity directly from Christ rather than being mediated by the clerical hierarchy.

Moreover, says Illanes, in Spain as in many other places then, there was a "strong tendency" to "identify the fullness of Christian life with the religious state." In practice, this meant that "life in the world, with all that involved in terms of everyday work, social relationships, and family life, was viewed very much as an obstacle to holiness." True, some earlier Catholic writers—St. Francis de Sales, for example—had understood that God's grace was fungible: a man or woman could become a saint while living a secular life and doing secular work, as well as by living a consecrated life in a monastery or convent. But even so, "the general view was that holiness in the world was... something very exceptional."

And here was this unknown priest named Josemaría Escrivá brashly claiming otherwise!

Although he lacked material resources, the young man had seemingly limitless resources of faith and trust. On August 7, 1931, as he was celebrating Mass, something happened that he recorded in his notes in these words: "At the moment of elevating the Sacred Host... there came to my mind, with extraordinary force and clarity, the phrase of Scripture *'et si exaltatus fuero a terra, omnia traham ad me ipsum'* [And I, if I am lifted up from the earth, will draw all things to myself] (Jn 12:32).... And I understood that it would be the men and women of God who would lift the Cross with the doctrines of Christ over the pinnacle of all human activity.... And I saw our Lord triumph, drawing to himself all things."

With encouragement like that, he struggled to launch Opus Dei. Leaving the chaplaincy of the Foundation for the Sick in order to devote more time to the effort, he joined a group of young laymen who made visits to charity patients in hospitals; at the same time, he taught catechism to children in the city's slums. He wrote in his Intimate Notes: "Children and the sick: When I write these words—'Child,' 'Sick'—I am tempted to capitalize them, because, for a soul in love, they are Christ." Later he was to say that for Opus Dei these years, like the years of the civil war that lay ahead, were a time for "growing on the inside."

But the visible growth was slow. When St. Josemaría gave his first study circle for students in January, 1933, only three showed up. He didn't allow himself to become discouraged. "What a flop, you're thinking? Well, it wasn't at all. I was very happy." As he gave benediction to those three young men, "to me it seemed that the Lord was blessing not three, nor three thousand, nor three hundred thousand, nor three million: he was blessing a whole multitude of people."

Gradually a handful of young followers and friends gathered around the charismatic priest—the Argentinian engineer Isidoro Zorzano, a medical student named Juan Jimenez Vargas, architecture student Ricardo Fernando Vallespin, and a few more. These were the first members of Opus Dei. More students started coming to study circles or seeking him out for spiritual counsel and confession. Soon the group needed its own base of operations.

The result, as 1933 drew to a close, was an establishment called the DYA Academy, situated in a four-bedroom apartment near the University of Madrid. St. Josemaría and his friends had hardly any money, but they did have an abundance of hope. "DYA" stood for the Spanish words for Law and Architecture, subjects the academy proposed to teach for a fee; but to Father Josemaría and the others they also stood for *Dios y Audacia*—God and Daring.

YEARS OF WAR

"Few conflicts in the twentieth century have stirred political consciences and fired literary imaginations as much as the Spanish Civil War." Thus a British journalist, a long-time resident of Spain, opens his review of yet another book on that momentous conflict. In 1936–39, he writes, Spain was "a country at war with itself as well as a stage on which a wider ideological and religious struggle was played out."

It was also the place where Opus Dei struggled to stay alive.

Hugh Thomas calls Spain on the eve of the civil war a country "constructed on quarrels," where "no habits of organization, compromise, or even articulation [were] respected, or even sought, by all. Insofar as there were traditions common to all Spain, these were of disputes." In general elections held in February 1936, the victory of a left-wing Popular Front coalition touched off a fresh wave of revolutionary and anticlerical violence by groups even farther to the left. In July, after months of indecision and plotting, the army finally moved, and on the 17th of July, a day earlier than intended, a long-anticipated uprising got underway among units in Spanish Morocco.

Fifty churches went up in flames in Madrid the night of July 19–20. As control slipped out of the Republican government's hands, the militias of revolutionary parties, particularly the communists, took to the streets. By this time, the DYA Academy had moved to quarters on Ferraz Street, near the Montana Barracks. Father Escrivá and several friends were there when fighting broke out, and they watched the bloody battle in horror. As the fortress fell to its attackers and the defenders were slaughtered, the priest donned blue overalls and slipped out of the apartment with the others. "A bad night, hot," he recorded in his Intimate Notes that day. "All three parts of the rosary.—Don't have my breviary.—Militia on the roof."

Religious persecution was soon in full swing, not only in Madrid but in other places where Republican forces or the anarchist, socialist, and communist militias who were the Republic's most active and effective early defenders held sway. As the struggle turned into a war of attrition, the persecution slacked off, but at no time in the next three years did it cease.

Much has been written about this war, and disagreements persist about what happened and who was to blame.

One thing certain is that large numbers of foreigners went to Spain in these years to assist one side or the other, and Germany, Italy, and the Soviet Union supplied important military aid to their respective Spanish clients of the right and the left.

George Orwell, future author of *Animal Farm* and *1984* and a man of the anti-Stalinist left, served with a dissident communist military unit on the Aragon front from late 1936 until he was seriously wounded in mid-1937. In a book about his experiences, *Homage To Catalonia*, published in late 1937, Orwell dismisses as a "pitiful lie" the claim that leftists attacked churches only if they were used as bases by Nationalist forces.

"Actually churches were pillaged everywhere and as a matter of course," Orwell reports, "because it was perfectly well understood that the Spanish Church was part of the capitalist racket. In six months in Spain I only saw two undamaged churches, and until about July 1937 no churches were allowed to reopen and hold services, except for one or two Protestant churches in Madrid." The author's own biases are in full view in his reference to the Church as "part of the capitalist racket," but what he says leaves little doubt that systematic attacks on churches did take place.

Brutality and atrocities on both sides marked the war. Numbers remain in dispute. According to one credible set of figures, there were 70,000 executions in the Republican zone and 40,000 in the Nationalist zone, with another 30,000 executions carried out by the Franco government from the end of the war until 1950. These deaths were over and above the hundreds of thousands of soldiers killed in the fighting. Among Church personnel, the executed included twelve bishops (including the bishops of Jaen, Lerida, Segorbe,

Cuenca, Barcelona, Almeria, Guadix, Ciudad Real, Tarragona, and Teruel, and the apostolic administrators of Barbastro and Orihuela), 283 religious sisters and nuns, 4,184 priests, and 2,365 religious men. One estimate of the overall death toll is mirrored in the title of a well-known novel: *One Million Dead*.

Historian Michael Burleigh calls the killing of clergy and religious "the worst example of anticlerical violence in modern history," surpassing even the French Revolution. "There was no evidence that the clergy had aided the military uprising, nor that houses of God were misused as rebel arms dumps," he notes. As for claims that the Church in Spain had "brought this catastrophe on its own head," Burleigh remarks: "Even then it was fashionable to blame the victims."

Confinement and Escape

After the war broke out, Father Escrivá at first took refuge in his mother's home, then, hoping to escape detection, moved about among the apartments of friends. Sometimes he was simply on the street. One day a man who looked like him was lynched outside the building where he was staying. A doctor who was a friend from Logroño provided him a hiding place in a mental asylum, where he remained for some weeks. In March, 1937, the Honduran consulate took him in, and he joined close to a hundred other people already there. His situation was not uncommon. Altogether, some 13,000 refugees sought safety in embassies and consulates in Madrid during the war.

Living conditions in the consulate were difficult. The place was badly overcrowded: St. Josemaría and his friends occupied a single room on a hallway where more than thirty people were living. The food was poor and sparse. Time hung heavy on people's hands, with boredom, tension, and fear gnawing at everyone. Writing to Opus Dei members in Valencia, Father Josemaría provided a semi-humorous but realistic description of the accommodations:

> There isn't room to spread out all five of our mattresses. Four are enough to completely carpet the floor. . . . When camp is struck, we have two mattresses, one on top of the other, folded up and put in one corner, the blankets and pillows tucked inside. Then a small space. Then the two mattresses of Jose B. and Alvaro, arranged in the same way, and on top of them, rolled up very tightly, with a funereal black cloth to cover it, Eduardo's thin mattress.
>
> Immediately adjacent is the radiator—five wheezing elements—on top of which is a board from a chest of drawers. This serves as a table for our food supplies and for six big cups, only superficially clean. One window, which looks out on a dark patio—very dark. Beneath the window, a small packing crate, with some books and a bottle for the banquets [with a suitcase or two placed on top, the crate became an altar for celebrating Mass]. . . .
>
> Although we have now reached the door, I won't make you leave the room. (You can enter whenever you like—the door doesn't shut; there's something wrong with it.) The only thing left for you to admire is the rope that cuts across a corner of the room and serves to hold five towels. And also the beautiful lampshade, of genuine newspaper. . . . Don't even think about touching the light switch, because if you do it will be a lot of trouble to get the light back on; the switch is broken.

The priest faced up to the challenge of sustaining morale by setting a daily schedule for himself and the others: Mass, with a homily or later a talk, prayer, reading, study, conversation. It worked. Later one of those young men wrote: "Sometimes we thought, If only this could last forever! Had we ever known anything better than the light and warmth of that little room? As absurd as it was in those circumstances, that was our reaction, and from our way of seeing things it made perfect sense. It brought us peace and happiness day after day."

Father Escrivá's fundamental spirit during this difficult time is suggested by a letter dated April 29, 1937, which he sent to members of the Work on the outside, using the guise of an elderly businessman writing to family members about the family business in order to confuse the censors: "My young ones! I can see that this business will in the near future be such a marvelous venture that it would be foolish for anyone to let this opportunity to be rich and happy slip away. How right they are to say that when one reaches seventy (and I'm eighty), one's greed increases! I long to see all of you gilded by the rays of the Sun, my loved ones radiating the pure gold acquired—very well acquired—by their efforts to make our family's patrimony grow." Here was a message filled with confidence for the future.

Finally, though, desperate for freedom of action, Escrivá and his friends left the consulate, traveled to Barcelona, and made the hazardous crossing out of the Republican zone over the Pyrenees into France, then back into the Nationalist zone. He spent 1938 in Burgos, the Nationalists' wartime capital, engaged in pastoral work, writing, and correspondence, making frequent trips to the front to visit his Opus Dei "sons" and other young men who, before the war, attended activities of Christian formation at DYA. As the long, exhausting war finally drew to a close, Father Josemaría Escrivá on March 27, 1939, hitched a ride in an army supply truck; and as the victorious troops entered Madrid, so did the priest, wearing his cassock. Later he was to write: "Never put up a cross just to keep alive the memory that some people have killed others. . . . Christ's Cross is to keep silent, to forgive and to pray for those on both sides, so that all may attain peace."

Later that year *The Way* was published. We turn next to the story of how, in the face of opposition from some Catholics, social upheaval, war, personal hardships, and danger, St. Josemaría managed to write the book.

CHAPTER THREE

THE WRITING OF *THE WAY*

He called them "Catherines," intending thereby to salute St. Catherine of Siena, the fourteenth-century Dominican mystic famous for badgering the Pope to quit Avignon and return to Rome and for a letter-writing campaign undertaken in hopes of ending the Great Schism splitting the Church while two competing candidates—and, for a time, three—claimed to be sole, legitimately elected Vicar of Christ. St. Josemaría's Catherines were handwritten notes recording, among other things, insights and communications that he'd received from God. On October 2, 1928, as we saw, he was reviewing them in hopes of discerning God's will when suddenly he "saw" Opus Dei.

These early jottings have been called the "matrix" of *The Way*. Although Father Josemaría said comparatively little about the book, the documentation regarding its writing is voluminous and extremely detailed. Much of this information is contained in the monumental critical-historical edition of *Camino* by Father Pedro Rodriguez, and the present chapter draws heavily on that remarkable achievement of scholarly devotion.

In both human and historical terms, the writing of *The Way* makes a fascinating and sometimes moving story.

Start with the Catherines. Having scribbled something on one of the scraps of paper that he habitually carried with him for that purpose, the priest would polish it later and transfer it to a bound notebook of "*Apuntes Intimos*"—Intimate Notes. Eventually he filled nine such notebooks. "I have never kept a diary because I don't like it," he said shortly before his death in 1975, "but I have been taking notes, always under my confessor's command. There appear persons, stories of concrete events, notes of exercises of when I was young. . . . So there is much material—a lot, a lot."

The contents and tone of many are suggested by the notebook entry for September 8, 1931. The writer was twenty-nine at the time. The note describes something that had happened the day before:

> Yesterday, at three in the afternoon, I went to the sanctuary of the Church of the Foundation to pray for a little while in front of the Blessed Sacrament. I didn't feel like it, but I stayed there, feeling like a nincompoop. Some time, coming to, I thought, "Now you see, good Jesus, that if I am here, it is for you, to please you."
>
> Nothing. My imagination ran wild, far from my body and my will, just as a faithful dog stretched at the feet of his master sleeps, dreaming of running around and of hunting and of friends (dogs like himself), and gets fidgety and barks softly . . . but without leaving his master. That's how I was, exactly like a dog, when I noticed that without meaning to, I was repeating some Latin words which I had never paid any attention to and had no reason to recall.
>
> Even now, to remember them, I have to read off the sheet of paper I always carry in my pocket for writing down whatever God wants. (Right there in the sanctuary, I jotted down that phrase instinctively on that sheet of paper out of habit, without attaching any importance to it.) The words of

Scripture that I found on my lips were, *Et fui tecum in omnibus ubicumque ambulasti, firmans regnum tuum in aeternum* [And I have been with you wherever you went ... your throne shall be established for ever (2 Sam 7:9, 16)]. Repeating them slowly, I applied my mind to their meaning.

Such experiences apparently weren't uncommon—the notes describe a number of them. In the mid-1930s, St. Josemaría burned the first of the notebooks, apparently troubled at the thought that a detailed record of these divine interventions might lead someone else to suppose that he was somebody special. Students of his life and thought can be grateful that the other eight notebooks were allowed to survive.

The jottings fall into four categories: those dealing with the spirit, mission, and structure of Opus Dei; those of an autobiographical nature, often recording intimate spiritual occurrences; those that report everyday events and activities—visits, pastoral work, family concerns, incidents on the street; and—particularly relevant to the writing of *The Way*—"considerations" that draw on the other three categories and contain practical lessons for Christian life. Later, many notes of this last kind, virtually unchanged, were to become points in his book.

Consideraciones Espirituales

On December 27, 1932, St. Josemaría finished the text for a 17-page pamphlet that was published the following month as *Consideraciones Espirituales*, "Spiritual Considerations." It is here that the publishing history of *The Way* begins.

The pamphlet doesn't carry its author's name, which was how the author intended it, since he hadn't been writing for general consumption but only for his personal work of spiritual direction. The text was typewritten by the priest, on a highly imperfect typewriter, and reproduced by a primitive version of mimeograph.

These first *Consideraciones* consist of 246 "points" (actually 247, since two points were accidentally run together in the typing—an error corrected by the author in some copies of the pamphlet). The points were arranged thematically, with the last five drawn from entries that the author made in his notebook on the very day he finished writing.

In the early summer of 1933 Father Josemaría mimeographed a second set of 87 points for a pamphlet of seven pages. These points then also became part of the *Consideraciones Espirituales*, and like their predecessors were eventually incorporated into *The Way*.

In these years St. Josemaría was struggling to get Opus Dei off the ground. So far, only a handful of people had been exposed to his message about sanctity in the world and responded positively. One of them was Maria Ignacia Garcia Escobar, a young tuberculosis patient in King's Hospital in Madrid. She joined Opus Dei in April 1932, and was to die in September 1933. In her diary she wrote of waiting for the *Consideraciones Espirituales* "with holy impatience," and she received the pamphlet enthusiastically, especially its teaching on spiritual childhood. Another early reader was Isidoro Zorzano, the engineer from Argentina. He wrote Escrivá of feeling a "serenity of spirit" when reading the *Consideraciones* that helped him see more clearly "the problems of my soul" while also getting his everyday activities in order. "How right you are," he declared, "when you say that to have his grace is to have . . . a third dimension."

Reactions like this started the author thinking: was there a real book here? He consulted his confessor, writing on the cover of a copy of the pamphlet that he sent this priest: "If they are seen to be useful, I'll put these notes in order later. For now they serve as a test."

The test was successful, and St. Josemaría moved on to the next stage. In 1934 the first printed predecessor of *The Way* appeared—a small book, also called *Consideraciones Espirituales*, printed on the elderly printing press of the diocesan seminary in Cuenca and published in that city. Its contents were the two earlier pamphlets plus 107 new points from Father Josemaría's sixth and seventh notebooks. A few points from the pamphlets were dropped. It is a peculiarity of the Cuenca edition that the points are not numbered. Considering what lay ahead, the major advance of this 1934 text was its division into 26 chapters that parallel the structure of the 46 chapters of *The Way*. The book-to-be had started to take shape.

With the 1934 version of the *Consideraciones* St. Josemaría began to contemplate the possibility of a wider audience. Thus he was at pains to revise points that up to now had referred specifically to Opus Dei in order to give them a general application. For example: the present no. 234 of *The Way*, which speaks of the nobility of suffering when undergone in the context of atonement (the original version in *Consideraciones* referred to suffering "in the Work of God"); and no. 915—"The works of God are not a lever, nor a stepping stone"—which originally had affirmed that "the Work of God" was neither of those things.

An incident during the preparation of the 1934 volume tells something about Father Escrivá's way of handling obstacles—in this case, an obstacle raised by a nervous bishop. Since he wasn't a priest of the Madrid diocese but was working there only by leave of the diocesan authorities, St. Josemaría considered it prudent not to stir things up by attempting to have his book published there. Instead he turned to an old friend, Father Sebastian Cirac, who lived in Cuenca, was close to its Ordinary, Bishop Cruz Laplana, and could be counted on to move things along by getting the Bishop's *imprimatur*—an official declaration of approval for publication—as canon law required.

Bishop Cruz was generally pleased with the manuscript, but one thing troubled him greatly. This was the author's praise for a spiritual trait that in several places he called "holy shamelessness"—a quality said to be fundamental to the "life of childhood" as it is lived by someone who's a child of God. Father Cirac wrote Father Josemaría that the Bishop wouldn't give an *imprimatur* to a book containing such a shocking expression, which "sounds bad and has a pejorative sense in conventional usage." Words like "resolution," "decision," and "courage" were suggested in its place. ("If you knew how much I suffer with these matters!" Father Cirac added plaintively.)

St. Josemaría put up a brief fight, but he quickly concluded that, one way or another, Bishop Cruz Laplana was sure to win. "The important thing is that [the book] be published, even if this means collaboration," he told his Intimate Notes. And so "holy shamelessness" became "holy daring." But the author made a prediction to himself: "The time will come when it can be published without alterations."

He was right. Nos. 387–391 in *The Way*, which open the chapter titled "Your Sanctity," shamelessly recommend holy shamelessness. "If you have holy shamelessness, you won't be bothered by the thought of what people have said or what

The Writing of *The Way*

they will say," no. 391 remarks. Perhaps Father Josemaría grinned at the thought that he was demonstrating the truth of that.

Consideraciones Espirituales was published in July 1934. "Brilliant and evangelically fruitful," Father Cirac pronounced. The author was identified only as "Jose Maria." A minimal 500 copies were printed, since St. Josemaría meant to use the book only in giving spiritual direction himself; although it carried a price—310 pesetas per copy—no commercial sales were planned.

Not surprisingly, considering the hostility to Opus Dei and St. Josemaría then present in some clerical circles in Madrid, a campaign against the book soon got underway. Writing in his notebook in October 1935, the priest reported being approached by a youth to whom he'd given a copy of *Consideraciones* a few days before; ingenuously, the young man asked him, "Father, this—the booklet—wouldn't be bad, would it?" The booklet's author concluded: "Jesus, I would like to write many books, but I understand that I will not have the time."

The Coming of the War

Time was indeed a problem for him now, but so were the troubled circumstances that then existed in Spain. Nevertheless, with tensions mounting and the fabric of society continuing to unravel, St. Josemaría labored to spread the message of sanctity in ordinary life.

Was he therefore indifferent to political events? Hardly. He saw what was happening, and he had his opinions. Like other priests, too, he sometimes came face-to-face with the hateful anticlericalism of the times acted out in crude and even menacing ways—a fistful of mud flung at the side of his head in the dark, a bricklayer who snarled as he passed, "A cockroach! It should be stepped on," other insults and assaults. And he suffered when others suffered. So, for instance, Parliament's severe measures against the Spanish Jesuits left him "physically exhausted and...infuriated." As the crisis heated up, he became increasingly anxious for the nation and for the Church.

St. Josemaría disliked super-patriots who exploited religion and had little patience with Catholics of questionable sincerity who flaunted their faith when it suited their purposes. "When you see people of doubtful professional reputation acting as leaders at public activities of a religious nature," he wrote, "don't you feel the urge to whisper in their ears: 'Please, would you mind being just a little less Catholic!'" (*The Way*, no. 371). It's safe to suppose he would have been appalled by the spectacle of ostentatiously Catholic politicians of the present day who declare themselves personally opposed to abortion—or to any other morally obnoxious practice—while opposing laws to prevent it.

To be sure, St. Josemaría believed that in the end faith really was the remedy for the ills of the world, but it had to be real faith lived out authentically, not the kind of faith that can be put on and taken off like an article of clothing to suit changes in the weather. "Have you ever bothered to think," he demanded, "how absurd it is to leave one's Catholicism aside on entering a university, or a professional association, or a scholarly meeting, or Congress, as if you were checking your hat at the door?" (*The Way*, no. 353). In saying this he anticipated a key insight of Vatican Council II: "One of the gravest errors of our time is the dichotomy between the faith which many profess and the practice of their daily lives"

(Pastoral Constitution on the Church in the Modern World, *Gaudium et Spes*, no. 43).

When the civil war broke out, Father Josemaría, like other priests, became a hunted man. Clerics' lives were now at risk as anticlerical militias roamed Madrid settling scores. Only in the Honduran consulate, starting in March 1937, did St. Josemaría enjoy a measure of precarious safety. We have seen how his disciplined regimen made life in that pressure-cooker atmosphere not just tolerable but spiritually fruitful for himself and his companions. And, perhaps even more remarkable, it was here that he started work on a new book.

Beginnings of *The Way*

From April to July of 1937 St. Josemaría wrote a hundred new points for what was to become *The Way*. Many originated in his homilies and meditations. The little group rose early in the morning, straightened the room, and rolled up their mattresses, which they then sat on while they prayed. After prayer, Father Josemaría preached, using the day's gospel as his theme. Mass followed. Varying this pattern, he occasionally spoke at night as part of a kind of prayer vigil before lights-out.

As soon as possible after he'd spoken, his remarks were recorded from memory by one of his companions, a young man named Eduardo Alastrue. Later the priest reviewed and corrected these semi-transcripts; and Zorzano, whose Argentine birth allowed him to move freely in the city, stopped by the consulate regularly in order to pick them up and circulate them among others on the outside.

In writing notes (which he now began calling *gaiticas*) for the proposed new book, St. Josemaría used the blank side of scraps of paper that had already been used on the other side. Years later, this habit, which he continued for the rest of his life, proved to be a godsend for researchers, who found this printed material a valuable guide to dating the notes.

The sources of numerous points in *The Way* are clearly visible in Alastrue's sketches of St. Josemaría's talks.

On April 6, 1937, for example, he said this: "How mistaken are those who claim they're ready for great sacrifices, heroic acts, when they can't conquer themselves in little things. They would gladly allow themselves to be crucified before a huge crowd in the center of Madrid, but are incapable of suffering the least pinprick." Very likely this was immediately relevant to persons and events in the physically cramped, emotionally strained conditions of the Honduran consulate. In no. 204 of the book it becomes: "Many who would let themselves be nailed to a cross before the astonished gaze of thousands of spectators won't bear the pinpricks of each day with a Christian spirit! But think, which is the more heroic?"

On May 15, criticizing something dubbed "confusionism"— defined as the indiscriminate fusion of error and truth—he referred to "people who seem to carry their heart around in their hands and offer it to everyone who passes by, saying, 'Who wants it?'" In the book this becomes: "You give me the impression you are carrying your heart in your hands, as if you were offering goods for sale. Who wants it? If it doesn't appeal to anyone, you'll decide to give it to God" (*The Way*, no. 146).

And in a meditation preached on June 21 we read, "All our fortitude is on loan," which in the book stands alone as no. 728.

We shall see more of these correspondences below.

Completion and Publication

After escaping with several companions from Republican Spain to the Nationalist zone in late 1937 and pausing in Pamplona to make a retreat, Father Josemaría reached Burgos on January 8, 1938. He first stayed briefly in a pension, then moved in late March to an undistinguished hotel called the Sabadell, where he and a few other members of the Work occupied a room with an alcove and a semi-private enclosed balcony. Using this modest site as his base of operations for the next nine months, the priest did pastoral work, traveled widely, and carried on an extensive correspondence.

He also worked on his new book. In the first eleven or twelve months in Burgos, proceeding at his customary pace, he composed another 139 points. Then, in a "big push" from December 20, 1938, to January 20, 1939, he produced 325 more. Typing the manuscript began on January 23. The final text is dated March 19, St. Joseph's Day.

As usual, his working conditions were far from ideal. Lacking elbow room, he spread scraps of paper with handwritten notes on his bed in order to experiment with different ways of organizing the material by shifting them around. "I wish I had a table as big as three beds," he remarked. Years later, asked if anyone helped him write *The Way*, he said, "No, nobody." But quickly he added, "Well, friends helped me arrange the notes on top of the bed."

From the start, he wanted the volume to look bright and appealing, in contrast with the dolorous black-covered prayer books of the time. Two young men, Pedro Casciaro and Miguel Fisac, were enlisted to work on the cover design. Since the book had 999 points, the first concept was a shower of 9's. Casciaro called that "more appropriate for a cookbook" and vetoed the idea. The final version nevertheless retained the "9" motif, with several large numerals making a striking appearance.

For months the author assumed that the name of the new book, like its predecessors, would be *Consideraciones Espirituales*. But some time between late April and the middle of May in 1939 that changed. One day, chatting with friends, he told them he'd abandoned *Consideraciones* as the title and was looking for something shorter and punchier. He mentioned several possibilities, but the only one his companions remembered later was *Camino*—"The Way." After a little more conversation, he announced that *Camino* would be the name. "He liked it, it was shorter, and it suited the cover," one of those present recalled.

A modest 2,500 copies of the book were printed in Valencia. A young man named Alfredo Sanchez Bella, two of whose brothers later became members of the Work, hand-carried the first ones to Madrid on the eve of October 2, 1939—eleventh anniversary of the founding of Opus Dei. Next day Escrivá went to the diocesan chancery office with two signed copies for the bishop.

The book went on sale in Valencia almost at once. Three weeks after publication, Sanchez Bella reported to Father Josemaría: "Sales go well here. We've already 'unloaded' about a hundred copies." A hundred copies! The author was pleased. "At the beginning," he said years later, "I thought we'd only sell three thousand copies in all. Now you see the result. It's more than human."

Still, not everything was sweetness and light for the new book. The number—999—stimulated strange fantasies among some of Opus Dei's critics.

The Writing of *The Way*

St. Josemaría liked the Trinitarian symbolism of 999. But rumors started to circulate that the number had esoteric significance known only to initiates of the Opus Dei cult. Father Josemaría was dismayed but also amused. In *Furrow*, a posthumously published book resembling *The Way*, the final point is numbered 1000. It reads: "I write this number so that you and I can finish this book with a smile, and so that those blessed readers who out of simplicity or malice sought a cabalistic significance in the 999 points of *The Way* may rest easier."

CHAPTER FOUR

UP THE INCLINED PLANE

In the view of at least one enthusiastic reader, *The Way*'s structure resembles that of a musical composition in four movements. Others may or may not agree. The author, St. Josemaría Escrivá, never said anything like that. While admitting that he'd found organizing the contents a bit of a chore, he expressed satisfaction with the results; but what the final plan was—how in his mind *The Way* really is organized—he never did say. Imaginative readers who find here a resemblance to a musical piece with four movements or to anything else are welcome to do that if they like.

Still, without definitively settling this question, the author did provide some hints. In a letter he said: "I wrote a good part of *Camino* in the years between 1928 and 1933, and published it in 1934 [this was the Cuenca edition of *Consideraciones Espirituales*]; and, with that publication, I tried to construct a very long inclined plane that souls would climb, little by little, gradually understanding God's call, until finally they became contemplative souls in the middle of the street."

Here's something for us to work with: the idea of a "very long inclined plane" to be ascended gradually by people attempting to understand, accept, and live out their vocations. In his monumental critical-historical edition of

Camino, Father Pedro Rodriguez makes use of this concept to tease out what he sees as the fundamental organizational structure of *The Way*. Its 46 chapters, he holds, are organized in three parts, with each part having two sections. The overall plan is this:

> **Part One:** To follow Christ—the beginning of the way (chapters 1–21). A) Prayer, atonement, examination (chapters 1–10). B) Interior life, work, love (chapters 11–21).
>
> **Part Two:** Toward sanctity—to walk *in ecclesia*, in the Church (chapters 22–35). A) Church, Eucharist, communion of saints (chapters 22–25). B) Faith, virtues, interior struggle (chapters 26–35).
>
> **Part Three:** Fully in Christ—calling and mission (chapters 36–46). A) Will and glory of God, spiritual childhood (chapters 36–42). B) Vocation and apostolic mission (chapters 43–46).

To repeat: this explanation of how *The Way* is organized isn't authoritative. Its source isn't the book's author but someone else. Readers of *The Way* will nowhere find indicators of a division into three parts, with two sections each; in fact, they won't even find numbered chapters. Those who believe they discern a structure different from this one are welcome to discern it. But, that said, Rodriguez's explanation does make sense, and it is offered here as help in analyzing and understanding the book.

As Father Rodriguez points out, following the hint provided by St. Josemaría in the letter mentioned above, the book's general plan didn't originate in Burgos during the final writing of *The Way* in 1938–39. Rather, it was worked out several years earlier, as Escrivá was preparing the *Consideraciones Espirituales* of 1934. *The Way* in its finished form contains much new material—in fact, it's more than twice the size of the 1934 volume; but the new material is integrated into a conceptual framework that dates back to 1934.

It's also important to be aware that the structure of *The Way* is not, and is not intended to be, that of traditional systematic theology (first, a general principle is stated, next it's explained, then come applications and illustrations and special cases, until the subject has been treated exhaustively in a highly logical way). Instead, as Rodriguez remarks, Escrivá's approach is "existential and practical." This is true of the overall plan of the book and also of the individual chapters, where ideas emerge, disappear, then surface again as the thought develops incrementally and dialectically. The analysis that follows will illustrate how that works in practice. Here the point is only that no one should approach *The Way* expecting to read a theology text. The book is altogether more dynamic and (with apologies to writers of theology texts) more exciting than that.

Traveling to Xanadu

Rodriguez's critical-historical edition of *Camino* and the several existing biographies of St. Josemaría Escrivá, especially the three-volume *The Founder of Opus Dei* by Andres Vazquez de Prada (published by Scepter), provide much information about the sources of *The Way* and the context in which it was written. All draw on the same archival material at Opus Dei headquarters in Rome.

I have no intention of repeating all that but, proceeding along the inclined plane, wish simply to offer a few indications concerning the book's historical and human background by looking at a relatively small number of its 999 points. Obviously someone can draw much benefit from *The Way* without knowing any of this, but the information that follows can enrich the reading of the book. Let me illustrate that point with an example from the field of literary studies.

Many years ago a volume popular among English professors and graduate students undertook to trace the sources of two extraordinary poems by the poet Coleridge: *The Rime of the Ancient Mariner* and *Kubla Khan*. Written by a British scholar named John Livingston Lowes and published in 1927, the book was called *The Road to Xanadu* (Xanadu being the place where, according to the poem, Kubla Khan built a sumptuous palace). Lowes's meticulous research demonstrated that the poet had mined—probably unconsciously in many cases—his broad and diverse reading in a number of more or less prosaic sources for materials that his creative imagination transmuted into exotic imagery.

Consider what follows a kind of Xanadu guide to *The Way*. As Rodriguez shows, St. Josemaría Escrivá also drew upon diverse sources. But unlike Coleridge, for whom, unconsciously or partially consciously, his sources were travel books and the like, Escrivá deliberately turned to his experiences with students, soldiers, bishops and priests, sick people, men and women in all social strata, and, most remarkable of all, to God's interventions in his life.

This helps make *The Way*, among other things, a sort of literary kaleidoscope filtering the rough-and-ready raw material of a particular time and place through the mind, heart, and sensibility of its author. Knowing something about the sources and the context of *The Way* can thus deepen our appreciation of an exceptional book as well as a great man of God.

St. Josemaría offered a few thoughts concerning the inclined plane in a homily in 1971. Before we start up it ourselves, let's pause and reflect on what he said.

> A Christian's struggle must be unceasing, for interior life consists in beginning and beginning again. This prevents us from proudly thinking that we are perfect already. It is inevitable that we should meet difficulties on our way. . . .
>
> We should not be surprised to find, in our body and soul, the needle of pride, sensuality, envy, laziness and the desire to dominate others. This is a fact of life, proven by our personal experience. It is the point of departure and the normal context for winning in this intimate sport, this race toward our Father's house. . . .
>
> To begin or sustain this conflict a Christian should not wait for external signs or nice feelings. Interior life does not consist in feelings but in divine grace, willingness and love. . . . Jesus Christ our Lord was moved as much by Peter's repentance after his fall as by John's innocence and faithfulness. Jesus understands our weakness and draws us to himself on an inclined plane. He wants us to make an effort to climb a little each day.

Let us begin.

Part One: To Follow Christ (Chapters 1–21)

Section One: Prayer, Atonement, Examination (chapters 1–10)

The first part of *The Way* is by far the longest, covering about half of the entire book. It lays out a demanding program. Reading and meditating on this material, one is reminded of St. Josemaría's comment that the book is intended for people "who really *want* to have interior life." The first section, dealing with prayer, atonement, and examination, examines conditions necessary for starting up the inclined plane—that is, for beginning to cultivate the life of the spirit. It consists of ten chapters: Character, Direction, Prayer, Holy Purity, Heart, Mortification, Penance, Examination of Conscience, Resolutions, and Scruples. Altogether, 264 points are covered.

The first chapter, Character (nos. 1–55), goes directly to the heart of the challenge for every Christian: "Don't let your life be sterile. Be useful. Blaze a trail. Shine forth with the light of your faith and of your love. With your apostolic life wipe out the slimy and filthy mark left by the impure sowers of hatred. And light up all the ways of the earth with the fire of Christ that you carry in your heart" (no. 1).

"God and daring"—the submerged motto of Escrivá's DYA Academy—makes its appearance in point no. 11. "*Regnare Christum volumus*—'We want Christ to reign!'" This was a revolutionary message to address to Catholic lay people in 1930s Spain, and, to a considerable extent, it's still revolutionary today.

The next point makes it clear that Escrivá understood the magnitude of the unique challenge facing him personally in attempting to begin Opus Dei. The origin of the point was a spiritual communication which he received on Saturday, December 12, 1931.

He was having lunch at the home of friends when some Latin words started running through his head and he spoke them aloud. Later he recorded the words in his notebook, observing that he'd "several times had those words on my lips these days" without paying much attention to them. Now he understood: "They are a promise that the W. of G. [Work of God] will overcome the obstacles; that the waters of its apostolate will flow through all the obstacles that present themselves." Here is how *The Way* expresses it: "Let obstacles only make you bigger. The grace of our Lord will not be lacking: *Inter medium montium pertransibunt aquae!*—'Through the very midst of the mountains the waters shall pass' [Psalm 104:10]. You will pass through mountains! What does it matter that you have to curtail your activity for the moment, if later, like a spring which has been compressed, you'll advance much farther than you ever dreamed?" (no. 12)

Chapter two (nos. 56–80) is titled Direction. At first it may be surprising to find spiritual direction treated at the start of the book, in the section presumably aimed especially at beginners. After all, isn't spiritual direction a refinement of the spiritual life intended for people who've advanced well beyond the beginner stage?

Escrivá saw the question very differently. Based on his experience, he saw that beginners need direction precisely because they *are* beginners and without sound guidance are at risk of wandering off and getting lost. No. 56 suggests as much: "The 'stuff' of saints. That's what is said about some people—that they have the stuff of saints. But apart from the fact that saints are not made of 'stuff,' having 'stuff' is not sufficient. A great spirit of obedience to a director and a great readiness to correspond to grace are required."

The chapter also says much about the respect due to priests—hardly surprising, considering the vicious anticlericalism rampant in Spain in those days. Moreover, Escrivá, despite his strong appreciation of the laity and healthy dislike of clericalism, also felt strongly that respect for the clergy was necessary for effective pastoral ministry by priests. Indeed, as a twenty-something priest, he'd remarked that he wished for the dignity that comes with being eighty.

Father Jose Maria Somoano, chaplain at King's Hospital in Madrid, met St. Josemaría in January 1932. He appears in *The Way* as a "saintly young priest" greatly distressed by sacrilegious communions. He died in July 1932, perhaps poisoned by some anticlerical staff member at his hospital.

St. Josemaría Escrivá in a photo from 1932. In these years the young priest, lacking human resources, was struggling against odds to launch Opus Dei as God wanted him to do. In an illumination while celebrating Mass on August 7, 1931, he wrote, "I saw our Lord triumph."

Bronze plaque from the DYA Academy, which Father Josemaría and a few friends established in 1933 in a four-bedroom apartment near the University of Madrid as a center for apostolic activity. "DYA" stood for the Spanish words for law and architecture, subjects taught at the academy. But to the priest and his companions, it also stood for *Dios y Audacia*—God and Daring.

This building was the first home of the DYA Academy. The pastoral work which St. Josemaría did there among students and other young people won him a growing following and served as a rich source of material for *The Way*.

Lola Fisac was one of the first women members of the Work. Concerned about her physical isolation from other members during the civil war, Father Josemaría counseled her to "live a special Communion of the Saints" (*The Way*, no 545). After the war she labored mightily for the rebirth of the women's branch of Opus Dei.

King's Hospital in Madrid. St. Josemaría spent long hours here engaged in pastoral ministry, and his experiences are reflected in many places in *The Way*. "Children and the sick," he once said. "When I write these words—'Child,' 'Sick'—I am tempted to capitalize them, because, for a soul in love, they are Christ."

The Honduran consulate in Madrid where St. Josemaría and several companions—along with a hundred other refugees—stayed at the height of the Spanish civil war. A significant portion of *The Way* had its origin in homilies and talks given here by the founder of Opus Dei.

The photo shows the church attached to the Foundation for the Sick, a charitable institution operated by the Apostolic Ladies of the Sacred Heart. Father Josemaría became chaplain here soon after his arrival in Madrid in 1927, and it was here that he offered Mass daily for the nuns, the sick and poor of the Foundation, and people of the neighborhood.

After escaping from the Republican zone over the Pyrenees, St. Josemaría spent 1938 and part of 1939 in Burgos, the Nationalists' wartime capital, engaged in pastoral work, making trips to the front to minister to young men serving there, and writing. Much of *The Way* was written here, in the Sabadell Hotel (right side of picture), where he lived for nine months. He and his companions occupied the room immediately above the entrance.

Another shot of the Foundation for the Sick. In time, Father Josemaría's chaplaincy became a base of operations for his steadily expanding pastoral and apostolic activities.

Another view of King's Hospital, where the young priest spent many long hours in a ministry later reflected in *The Way*.

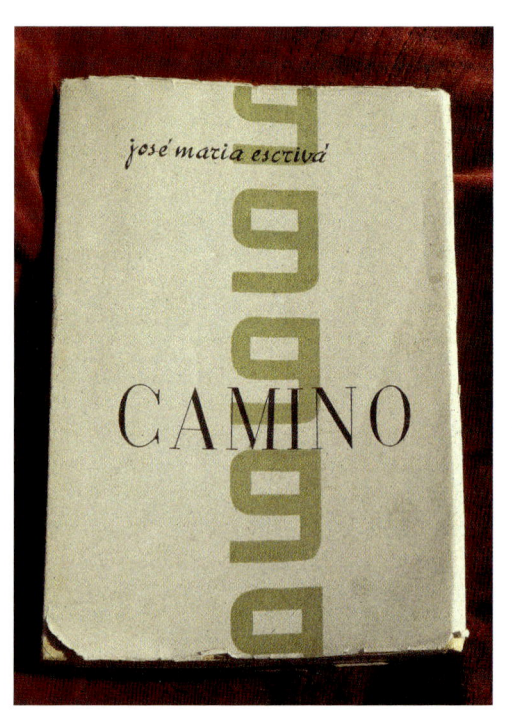

Father Escrivá wanted *The Way* to look as little as possible like the dolorous black-bound devotional books common in his day, so two young members of the Work were commissioned to design the cover. The result, seen in this photo of the first edition, was a book of striking appearance whose cover with its '9' motif recalled the 999 "points" inside. The volume was printed in Valencia in a first edition of 2,500 copies.

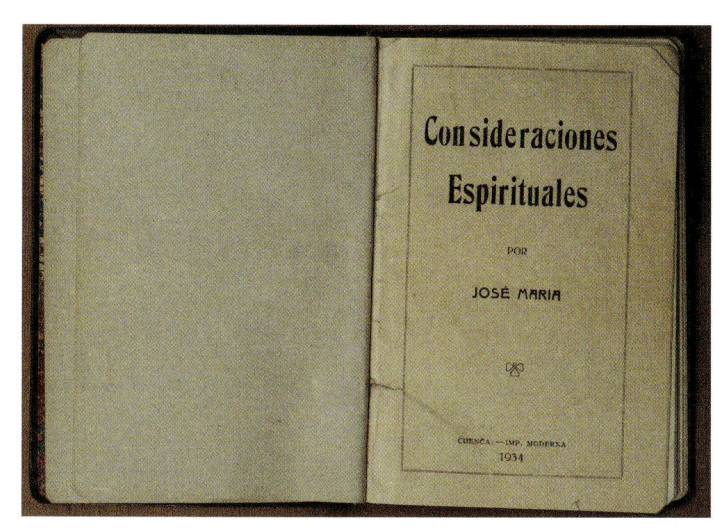

The immediate predecessor of *The Way* was *Consideraciones Espirituales* (Spiritual Considerations), published in 1934 in Cuenca. Its 26 chapters resemble the organizational plan of *The Way*'s 46, and much of its contents appear in the later book. The *Consideraciones* had a printing of only 500 copies, intended by the author for use only in giving spiritual direction himself. After he began work on *The Way*, St. Josemaría took it for granted that it, too, would be called *Consideraciones Espirituales*, and it did not receive its new title until the spring of 1939, a few months before its publication in the fall.

Although this was not the typewriter used by St. Josemaría in writing *The Way*, it seems likely that he did use one very much like it. As for this particular machine, the plaque in the photo identifies it as one that he and Don Alvaro del Portillo, his successor as head of Opus Dei, used in preparing documents for the Holy See in giving its approval to the Work.

Luis Gordon, manager of a family-owned factory, was one of a group of young men whom St. Josemaría accompanied in 1931–32 on Sunday afternoon visits to Madrid's General Hospital. In a touching incident recorded in *The Way* (no. 626), while cleaning out a bedpan he was overheard to say, "Jesus, may I put on a happy face!" Soon after asking to join Opus Dei and not long after the death of Father Jose Maria Somoano, Luis Gordon unexpectedly died. The two deaths were a heavy blow to Father Escrivá, who accepted them as God's will.

Another favorite theme of his turns up here: the importance of order as an ascetical discipline. For example, no. 78: "If you don't get up at a set hour, you'll never fulfill your plan of life." (This sound piece of practical advice is familiar to the faithful of Opus Dei as the "heroic minute.") The chapter also contains one of the several historically conditioned remarks in *The Way* that today's reader is likely to find rather odd: "When a layman sets himself up as an arbiter of morals, he frequently errs; laymen can be only disciples" (no. 61). Now, of course, there are many distinguished lay scholars in ethics and moral theology. Arising from a suggestion by the author's Jesuit confessor, the point reflects the fact that moral theology at that time was mainly a seminary course preparing future priests to hear confessions.

Chapter three, Prayer (nos. 81–117), speaks of another absolute requirement of the spiritual life. "You don't know how to pray?" Father Josemaría must have often heard that lament from the young people he worked with in the early days. He responds with advice he undoubtedly gave many times: "Put yourself in the presence of God, and as soon as you have said, 'Lord, I don't know how to pray!' you can be sure you've already begun" (no. 90).

No. 110 provides an intimate glimpse of the author's own experience of prayer. It dates back at least to 1931, when he began to be aware that he could hardly start to read a newspaper before thoughts of God intruded. As time went by, he realized that he was visited by both spiritual dryness and the sense of God's presence according to a timetable that plainly wasn't his. In a notebook entry dated March 26, 1932, he wrote: "I know someone who feels cold (despite his faith, which is limitless) near the divine fire of the tabernacle, and then later, in the middle of the street, amid the noise of automobiles and streetcars and people—when reading a newspaper!—is seized with mad raptures of love for God."

As often, in making this experience a part of *The Way* Escrivá suppresses the fact that he's speaking of himself. "You told me once that you feel like a broken clock that strikes at the wrong time; you're cold, dry and arid at the time of your prayer. And, on the other hand, when you least expect it, on the street, in your everyday tasks, in the midst of the noise and hustle of the city or in the concentrated calm of your professional work, you find yourself praying.... At the wrong time? Possibly; but don't let those chimes of your clock go to waste. The Spirit breathes where he pleases" (no. 110).

Chapter four considers Holy Purity (nos. 118–145). As with the decision to speak of direction in the second chapter, here, too, someone might question the decision to treat purity at this early stage of the inclined plane, rather than later in the several chapters devoted to other virtues (faith, humility, obedience, etc.). The answer may upset some people today, when sins against chastity often are treated as if they were of little importance or weren't even sins. Like a lot else in Escrivá's understanding of the spiritual life, however, the approach adopted here reflects a realistic view of the human condition: there's simply no possibility of progress in the spiritual life for someone paralyzed by habitual, semi-compulsive sins of impurity. Isolated sins—yes, a person can hope to struggle successfully with them; but repeated, unresisted surrenders to sensuality—no. "Without holy purity," the author pronounces flatly, "you can't persevere in the apostolate" (no. 131).

The chapter closes with a vivid anecdote from the days of the civil war. Ricardo Fernandez Vallespin recounted the incident in a letter to Father Josemaría in December 1938. In *The Way* it goes like this:

> The battlefront in Madrid. A score of officers in noble and cheerful camaraderie. A song is heard, then another, and another...
>
> That young lieutenant with the brown moustache heard only the first one:
>
> I do not like
> divided hearts;
> I give mine whole,
> and not in parts.
>
> "What a struggle to give my whole heart!" And a prayer flowed forth in a calm, broad stream (no. 145).

Next comes an entire chapter called Heart (nos. 146–171). Escrivá was sensitive to the spiritual implications of the affective side of life. Here he speaks of both positive and negative aspects, the pluses and the minuses of heart. No. 168 repeats something the Bishop of Avila, a friend, told Escrivá about Escrivá himself in a letter of 1938: "It made me laugh to hear you speak of the 'account' our Lord will demand of you. No, for you he will not be a judge—in the harsh sense of the word. He will simply be Jesus." To which the author adds: "These words, written by a holy bishop, have consoled more than one troubled heart and could very well console yours."

"Love... is well worth any love!" he sums up (no. 171). This thought recurs throughout his writing, including the homilies and meditations from the Honduran consulate.

The next two chapters are devoted to Mortification (nos. 172–207) and Penance (nos. 208–234). Practices of mortification and penance, ignored in much that's said and written about the spiritual life today, occupy a central place in Escrivá's thinking. His own mortification was famously strenuous, although he acted under the guidance of spiritual directors and did what he deemed appropriate and necessary for himself, without requiring or even allowing others to imitate him. No. 197 speaks of the situation in the Sabadell Hotel in Burgos, where the priest, occupying an alcove curtained off from the rest of the room, made vigorous use of the discipline: "If they have witnessed your weaknesses and faults, does it matter if they witness your penance?"

As a practical matter, though, Escrivá didn't call for dramatic acts of penance and mortification but for patient acceptance of everyday tribulations, both those that generous people voluntarily impose on themselves and those that come to everyone unsought. Earlier we saw his dismissive opinion of people who could daydream about being hung on a cross in downtown Madrid but couldn't bear the daily pinpricks of life in the Honduran consulate; this becomes no. 204 of *The Way*.

The same thought—the ascetical value of small, everyday mortifications—appears again in no. 205. In a letter of June 1938 Escrivá speaks of an Irish Jesuit, Father William Doyle, who served as an army chaplain and died in August 1917 in the battle of Ypres: apparently he'd been reading the dead priest's biography and was impressed by his "heroically ordinary life," including his daily struggle, painstakingly recorded, not to take butter at meals. "One day at breakfast he would win, the next day he'd lose... 'I didn't take butter... I did take butter!' he would jot down. May we too—you and I—live our... 'drama' of the butter." (It's said that when an Irish edition of *The Way* was in preparation, those responsible believed Irish readers would find the notion of not putting butter on their toast and scones virtually incomprehensible and therefore suggested that marmalade be substituted for butter. The translators were unaware that St. Josemaría was, in fact, speaking of an Irishman. It required the intervention of Alvaro del Portillo, on a trip to Ireland, to keep the drama of the butter intact in the Emerald Isle.)

Is fretting about butter simply an exercise in trivia? Not when it is seen in the larger context proposed in *The Way*: "Blessed be pain. Loved be pain. Sanctified be pain. . . . Glorified be pain!" (no. 208). Father Josemaría prayed those words in a Madrid charity hospital with a dying woman—a "camp follower" whom he converted—and they found their way into his Intimate Notes written on January 14, 1932, and then into his book. Pain, in his view, wasn't valuable for its own sake; following the wisdom of the ascetical tradition, he saw it instead as a means of reparation and spiritual growth, and he encouraged others to see it and use it as such. "Atonement: this is the path that leads to life," he affirmed (*The Way*, no. 210).

A chapter on Examination of Conscience (nos. 235–246) is followed by Resolutions (nos. 247–257), since these are natural products of honest self-examination. "Be specific," Escrivá insists. "Don't let your resolutions be like fireworks that sparkle for an instant, only to leave as bitter reality a blackened, useless butt that is disgustedly thrown away" (no. 247).

Resolutions are essential for anyone who wants to avoid the sandbag syndrome. From the first, Father Josemaría used this image to lambaste halfhearted apathy about the things of God. One of those who attended his conferences in the early 1930s recalls: "It was impossible for us to remain a spectator when the Father preached. He personally prayed aloud and drew us into his prayer.... He would remind us not to sit there like bags of sand but to speak to God on our own." In *The Way* we read: "You drag along like a sandbag. You don't do your share. No wonder you are beginning to feel the first symptoms of lukewarmness. Wake up!" (no. 257).

And so, after a short chapter on the unpleasant topic of Scruples (nos. 258–264)—obviously related to the chapters on direction and examination—the first stretch of the inclined plane draws to a close.

SECTION TWO: INTERIOR LIFE, WORK, LOVE (CHAPTERS 11–21)

Section two of part one examines the conditions for continued progress in the interior life on the part of someone who's begun to make the necessary effort. Its eleven chapters are: Presence of God, Supernatural Life, More About Interior Life, Lukewarmness, Study, Forming the Spirit, Your Sanctity, Love of God, Charity, The Means, and Our Lady. The 251 points in this section make up just over a fourth of the total in *The Way*.

Presence of God (nos. 265–278) speaks of something Escrivá saw to be crucial: "It's necessary to be convinced that God is always near us. Too often we live as though our Lord were somewhere far off—where the stars shine. We fail to realize that he is also by our side—always" (no. 266). As always, rather than leave this as a pious generalization, he is concrete, urging a variety of specific practices—short prayers frequently repeated throughout the day, pictures of the Virgin Mary and the saints, a small crucifix on your desk or in your pocket—to supply constant reminders of the divine in every setting and circumstance.

For the faithful of Opus Dei one of the most familiar of these reminders is a black wooden cross without the figure of the crucified Christ. "You ask me, 'Why that wooden cross?' And I quote from a letter: 'As I raise my eyes from the microscope, my sight comes to rest on the cross—black and empty. That cross without a corpus is a symbol; it has a meaning others won't see. And I, tired out and on the point of abandoning my work, once again bring my eyes close to the lens and continue. For that lonely cross is calling for a pair of shoulders to bear it' " (no. 277).

This is from a letter written on May 4, 1938, by Jimenez Vargas, then serving as a medical officer on the Teruel front. But the black wooden cross made its first appearance much earlier—at the DYA Academy, in Father Escrivá's study and then outside the oratory. Its symbolism, recalled here by an army doctor, is that every follower of Christ must do his or her part to carry on the work of redemption by shouldering the cross as it takes shape in his or her life. A black wooden cross without the corpus still hangs outside every oratory in every Opus Dei center around the world.

Next come two linked chapters called Supernatural Life (nos. 279–300) and More About Interior Life (nos. 301–324).

Nearly four decades later Escrivá spoke of the early days, when he spent many hours visiting patients in charity hospitals and children in city slums, as "intense years when Opus Dei was growing on the inside." That same image was also much on his mind as the civil war drew to a close. In a circular letter to members of the Work dated January 9, 1939, he acknowledeged that some might see the war years as a time when Opus Dei "came to a standstill." But, he insisted, "this Work of God is alive and kicking and does have fruitful activity going on, like a sown grain of wheat that is germinating under the frozen earth."

No. 294 similarly recalls long months of frustration and confinement and relates that experience to the interior life: "The plants were hidden under the snow. And the farmer, the owner of the land, remarked with satisfaction: 'Now they're growing on the inside.' I thought of you, of your forced inactivity. . . . Tell me, are you also growing on the inside?"

The war itself provided lessons and images. No. 307 speaks of a "real military strategy" in the spiritual struggle: "You carry on the war—the daily battles of your interior life—in positions far from the main walls of your fortress. And the enemy comes to meet you there: in your small mortification, in your daily prayer, in your orderly work, in your plan of life. And only with difficulty does he get close to the otherwise easily-scaled battlements of your citadel." The origin of this was a meditation preached in May 1937 in the Honduran consulate.

Lukewarmness gets a short chapter of seven points to itself (nos. 325–331). Around Christmas of 1938, while reorganizing his material, the author appears to have made the late decision to devote a separate chapter to this topic; but his concern with it dates back at least several years, and the first point on lukewarmness, no. 325, is identical to a notebook entry of January 5, 1934 ("Fight against the softness that makes you lazy and careless in your spiritual life . . .").

In its extreme form, the classical name for the spiritual sickness here called lukewarmness is *acedia* (or sometimes sloth). About it, the Catechism of the Catholic Church says this: "*Acedia* or spiritual sloth goes so far as to refuse the joy that comes from God and to be repelled by divine goodness" (#2094). Spiritual writers traditionally have seen it as one of the most serious obstacles to perfection.

In this context, Escrivá makes an important point about venial sin: "Venial sins do great harm to the soul. That's why our Lord says in the Canticle of Canticles: *Capite nobis vulpes parvulas, quae demoliuntur vineas*—'Catch the little foxes that destroy the vines'" (no. 329). That thought had been with him for a long time: a notebook entry of March 13, 1930, reads, "Lord, may I never knowingly offend you, not even venially."

As we know, Father Josemaría from the start reached out to university students for whom study was their work. So it's natural that Study now becomes a chapter—a long one consisting of 28 points (nos. 332–359). It is noteworthy that, in line with his emphasis on work's central place in the interior life, he should caution against substituting pious practices for study: "You pray, you mortify yourself, you labor at a thousand apostolic activities . . . but you don't study. You are useless, then, unless you change your ways. Study—any professional development—is a serious obligation for us" (no. 334).

But that also cuts the other way. Unless linked to interior life, academic and professional achievement do not count for a lot. "You worry only about building up your culture. But what you really need to build up is your soul. Then you will work as you should—for Christ. In order that he may reign in the world, it is necessary to have people of prestige who . . . dedicate themselves to all human activities . . ." (no. 347). As Escrivá saw in the critically important illumination that took place in the chapel of the Foundation of the Sick in August 1931, God wants "a handful of men 'of his own' in every human activity" in order to build up the kingdom of Christ.

Three closely related chapters come near the end of the second section of part one: Forming the Spirit (nos. 360–386), Your Sanctity (nos. 387–416), and Love of God (nos. 417–439).

In passing, one of the small anomalies in the history of *The Way* deserves mention. Through a mixup, points no. 381 and no. 940 were repeated in the first several editions. Not until 1948 did a translator discover the error and call it to the author's attention—whereupon the author wrote a new no. 381, thus making it the last point to be written. It reads: "Don't worry if people say you have too much *esprit de corps*. What do they want? A delicate instrument that breaks to pieces the moment it is grasped?" And no. 940 remains as it had been from the start: "Let us not forget that unity is a symptom of life; disunion is decay, a sure sign of being a corpse."

Having traveled this far up the inclined plane, the reader is entitled to suppose that the preliminaries are over, and from here on Escrivá will speak about elements of the interior life of someone who's passed beyond the beginner stage and is serious about becoming a saint. This is so, yet the book remains nuanced and realistic just the same.

Consider no. 394: "Compromising is a sure sign of not possessing the truth. When a man yields in matters of ideals, of honor or of faith, that man is without ideals, without honor, and without faith." A hard saying, to be sure. But observe that it comes from one of the Honduran consulate meditations, preached on April 12, 1937, in which Escrivá commends Zacchaeus, the little tax collector who didn't hesitate to shed his dignity and shinny up a tree for a look at Jesus. In a pinch, dignity can go: but not ideals, honor, and faith. Furthermore: "Holy steadfastness is not intolerance" (no. 396). Hence the conclusion: "Be steadfast in doctrine and in conduct, but pliant in manner: a powerful blacksmith's hammer wrapped in a quilted covering. Be steadfast, but don't be obstinate" (no. 397). This also comes from one of the consulate talks—the date was May 12, 1937—where the image of the blacksmith's hammer is preceded by the words *suaviter et fortiter* (pleasantly and firmly).

The ideal of "God and daring!"—motto of the DYA Academy—is cited several times in this section. But along with it, Father Josemaría underlines something else: "Daring is not imprudence. Daring is not recklessness" (no. 401). The model is the daring of someone in love: "Don't ask, tell him: 'Jesus, I want this or that.' For that's the way children ask" (no. 403).

St. Josemaría wasn't a spokesman for muscular Christianity. There is at times an almost feminine tenderness in his words. "Children . . . the sick . . . As you write these words, don't you feel tempted to write them with capitals? The reason is that in little children and in the sick, a soul in love sees him!" (no. 419). Taken from his Intimate Notes, March 11, 1932, this was his reaction to the experience of teaching catechism to poor children and visiting hospital patients.

Love of God naturally finds expression in "effusions of love and gratitude" (no. 434). One real-life effusion provides material for no. 438: "Mad! Yes, I saw you (in the bishop's chapel, you thought you were alone) as you left a kiss on each newly-consecrated chalice and paten, so that he might find it there when for the first time he would 'come down' to those eucharistic vessels." The "he" is Jesus, present in the consecrated species of bread and wine. The protagonist of this incident was Father Josemaría himself, who on

December 22, 1937, kissed the patens and chalices awaiting consecration in the chapel of the bishop's residence in Pamplona where he'd gone to make a retreat after escaping from the Republican zone.

Building on love of God, the nineteenth chapter, Charity (nos. 440–469), speaks of charity toward others in ordinary life—family, work, apostolic enterprises, and so on. Chapter twenty, The Means (nos. 470–491), written mostly in Burgos in 1938, speaks of what it takes to succeed in apostolate: "keen and living faith" (no. 489) together with "an upright heart and good will" (no. 490). Essentially these are graces, gifts of God.

Chapter twenty-one, Our Lady (nos. 492–515), brings part one to a close. Mary's role as Mother of the Church makes this an appropriate transition to the second part's treatment of ecclesial aspects of the interior life. It also reflects Escrivá's fervent devotion to the Blessed Virgin, as in no. 501: "When you were asked which image of our Lady aroused your devotion most, and you answered with the air of long experience, 'all of them,' I realized that you are a good son." This recalls an incident that occurred late in 1932. Coming across a dirt-smudged picture of the Virgin lying in the street, the priest picked it up and, as he did, suddenly intuited that it had been torn out of a catechism and flung away in contempt. "I will not burn the poor picture," he wrote in his Intimate Notes. "I will save it, and put it in a nice frame when I have the money." In December the money turned up, and he did as he'd promised, asking Mary to return the favor by finding him a place to teach catechism. Next month he was able to start doing that at a school run by sisters in a Madrid slum called Barriada de los Pinos.

PART TWO: TOWARD SANCTITY—TO WALK IN *ECCLESIA* (CHAPTERS 22–35)

SECTION ONE: CHURCH, EUCHARIST, COMMUNION OF SAINTS (CHAPTERS 22–25)

In the 1971 homily mentioned above, St. Josemaría refers to the ecclesial dimension of the interior life. Citing the Book of Revelation's words to the church of Sardis—"I know your works; you have the name of being alive, and you are dead. Awake..." (Rev. 3:1–2)—he links personal spirituality to life in the communion of the Church: "Nobody can save himself by his own efforts. Everyone in the Church needs specific means to strengthen himself: humility, which disposes us to accept help and advice; mortifications which temper the heart and allow Christ to reign in it; the study of abiding, sound doctrine which leads us to conserve and spread our faith." This could serve as a sketch of part two of *The Way*.

The first section begins with a chapter called The Church (nos. 517–527). Here the author speaks of the liturgy, a subject on which his views are clear, as found in an entry in his Intimate Notes of 1931: "Today, at a rich school, the altarpiece was filled with ridiculous artificial flowers set on steps of half-painted crate board. The tabernacle is usually set up in such a way that the priest... has to get up on a footstool to open and close it to take out our Lord.... He has to do Charleston-like pirouettes to avoid hitting his head on a hideous gilded brass lamp, which hangs very low over the sanctuary.... And the songs! They are such that one could say the Mass was not sung... but could have been danced to!"

The Way speaks something more important because more fundamental: "Show veneration and respect for the holy liturgy of the Church and for its ceremonies. Observe them faithfully. Don't you see that, for us poor humans, even what is greatest and most noble enters through the senses?" (no. 522).

Escrivá always called the eucharistic sacrifice "Holy Mass" (the title of the next chapter) and he took everything pertaining to it with the seriousness suitable to matters of faith and divine worship. No. 532 gives a picture of another such priest: "How that saintly young priest, who was found worthy of martyrdom, wept at the foot of the altar as he thought of a soul who had come to receive Christ in the state of mortal sin! Is that how you offer him reparation?"

This priest was Father Jose Maria Somoano, chaplain at King's Hospital, who met Father Escrivá in January 1932. Escrivá's notebook records the young man's grief in the face of sacrilegious communions. Father Somoano died in agony on the night of July 16, 1932. *The Way*'s reference to his "martyrdom" reflects the suspicion that he was poisoned—perhaps by someone on the rabidly anticlerical staff of the hospital where he worked. "I had put so much hope in his upright and energetic character," the founder of Opus Dei wrote. "God wanted him for himself."

Chapter 24, Communion of the Saints (nos. 544–550), takes it for granted that the reader is familiar with the Church's hierarchical structure. Less familiar to Escrivá's university students then (as it remains to many Catholics today) was the idea that the Church's nature as *communio* involves a sharing of responsibility for its mission on the part of all its members. This vision of the Church as communion is expressed here in words of advice addressed by Father Josemaría to one of Opus Dei's first women members, Lola Fisac.

Fisac, whose brother Miguel was one of Escrivá's companions in the crossing of the Pyrenees, declared her wish to join the Work in a letter written in May 1937. Living in the town of Daimiel in southern Spain, however, she was physically isolated from other members. Escrivá's counsel to her in these circumstances is reflected in two points in *The Way*: "Live a special Communion of the Saints, and at the moment of interior struggle, as well as during the long hours of your work, each of you will feel the joy and the strength of not being alone" (no. 545); and "You will find it easier to do your duty if you think of how many brothers are helping you, and of the help you fail to give them when you are not faithful" (no. 549). Later, after the civil war, Fisac was instrumental in the rebirth of the women's branch of Opus Dei.

Chapter twenty-five takes up the topic of Devotions (nos. 551–574) and continues the previous chapter's theme of *communio*: in this case, communion with the faithful in heaven and purgatory, communion with the angels, especially guardian angels, and communion with the Virgin Mary.

Escrivá sees devotional practices not merely as expressions of personal piety but also as means for building up and sustaining ecclesial communion. While cautioning against falling into a rut in using them (no. 551) or having too many of them (no. 552), he also strongly commends certain ones: devotion to the humanity of Christ and his wounds (no. 555), the Way of the Cross (no. 556), the Rosary, described as a "powerful weapon" (no. 558), devotion to St. Joseph as a "teacher of the interior life" (no.

560), friendship with one's guardian angel as a companion who "will do a thousand services for you in the ordinary affairs of each day" (no. 362).

He believed he had personal experience of those angelic services. After all, it was on the feast of the guardian angels, October 2, that he first "saw" Opus Dei. But, besides that, there also were occurrences like one recorded in his Intimate Notes, December 1932: "Yesterday my pocket watch stopped. This put me in a real bind, since it's the only watch I've got and since my *capital*, at the moment, amounts to seventy-five cents.... I talked this over with my Lord, and suggested that he have my guardian angel ... fix my watch." Kneeling down, the young priest started to say an Our Father and a Hail Mary. "I think I hadn't yet finished when I picked up the watch, touched the hands ... and it started running!"

Not surprisingly, the guardian angels get a generous nine points to themselves in *The Way*.

Section Two: Faith, Virtues, Interior Struggle (Chapters 26–35)

The next seven chapters deal with virtues: Faith (nos. 575–588), Humility (nos. 589–613), Obedience (nos. 614–629), Poverty (nos. 630–638), Discretion (nos. 639–656), Joy (nos. 657–666), and a miscellany of Other Virtues (nos. 667–684).

No. 626 (in the chapter on Obedience) speaks of the consolation Jesus must have taken from a remark made by a man who found himself "disconcerted by having to obey in something unpleasant and repulsive." The man was Luis Gordon, a businessman who managed a family-owned factory that processed malt for the beer industry. Gordon was one of several young men who spent Sunday afternoons visiting the sick poor in Madrid's General Hospital. Starting in November 1931 and continuing during the following year, Father Josemaría accompanied them.

Visiting the sick poor could be unpleasant work. One Sunday Gordon was with Father Josemaría while the priest tended a tuberculosis patient. Escrivá asked his companion to clean the bedpan, which was full of bloody phlegm. Saying nothing, Gordon picked up the receptacle and carried it to a bathroom. When Escrivá went to help him, the bedpan was in the sink while Gordon, sleeves rolled to his elbows, cleaned it by hand, saying quietly as he did, "Jesus, may I put on a happy face!"

Not long after, Luis Gordon asked to join Opus Dei. On November 5, 1932, the young man unexpectedly died. Coming so soon after Father Somoano's death in July, this was a particularly heavy blow to Father Josemaría's hopes. God, he wrote, had taken "the two best-prepared ones so that we would not put our trust in anything earthly, not even someone's personal virtues, but only and exclusively in his most loving Providence."

The Way also contains a few hints of the hostility and opposition that Escrivá and Opus Dei encountered in the early days—here, transformed into counsel for Christians whenever and wherever they're treated unjustly.

Chapter thirty-three, Tribulations (nos. 685–706), speaks obliquely of Opus Dei's "persecution by the good" that was to continue for years. Father Josemaría took the view that the same thing was likely to happen to anyone who was serious about following Christ. "Once again, they've been talking, they've written—in favor, against; with good, and with not so good will; insinuations and slanders, panegyrics and plaudits; hits and misses . . ." (no. 688). His advice was simple: "Your supernatural reaction should be to pardon—and even to *ask* for pardon!—and to take advantage of the experience to detach yourself from creatures" (no. 689).

There were many of these storms for Escrivá. One day in May of 1934 he dropped by the Madrid chancery on business and while there heard one chancery official say to another, "He's the one running that fundamentalist sect." Later he was informed that the chancery had received a letter containing allegations against the DYA Academy, and on May 28 he was summoned back to give his side of the story to the vicar general of the diocese. He gave it at length. When he finished, the vicar general asked him to work up a plan of religious studies for university students that the diocese could use.

"Cross, toil, tribulation: such will be your lot as long as you live," he wrote in *The Way*. "That was the way Christ followed, and the disciple is not above his Master" (no. 699). Something he told his companions in the Honduran consulate on June 21, 1937, is repeated in chapter thirty-four (Interior Struggle): Don't lose your nerve and always trust in God. In the end: "All our fortitude is on loan" (no. 728).

Part Three: Fully in Christ—Calling and Mission (chapters 36–46)

Section One: Will and Glory of God, Spiritual Childhood (chapters 36–42)

As the inclined plane leading to union with God enters its home stretch, the focus turns to Last Things (nos. 734–753). Traditionally, these are death, judgment, heaven, hell, and purgatory. The subject is a favorite one with saints. St. Thomas More, nearing the end, called death his companion on the journey of life. Sharing that perspective, St. Josemaría Escrivá speaks of death with Christian realism.

It was unavoidably on his mind in the Honduran consulate, with violent death on the streets of Madrid a common occurrence. No. 739 of *The Way* is drawn from a meditation preached on April 6, 1937: "Don't be afraid of death. Accept it from this day on, generously . . . when God wills it, how God wills it, where God wills it. Believe me, it will come at the time, in the place and in the way that are best—sent by your Father God. May our sister death be welcome!" A meditation on June 28 is the source of no. 741: "Do you see how the corpse of a loved one disintegrates in foul and reeking fluids? Well, that is the body beautiful! Contemplate it and draw your own conclusions." And no. 743 is from a letter written in the consulate on September 18 to members of the Work in Valencia: "You talk of dying 'heroically.' Don't you think that it is more heroic to die unnoticed, in a good bed, like a bourgeois . . . but to die of love?"

Chapters thirty-six, The Will of God (nos. 754–778), and thirty-seven, The Glory of God (nos. 779–789), form a unit. The central idea is stated in no. 755, which is drawn from a letter written in 1938 to a young man to whom he was giving spiritual direction: "Many great things depend—don't forget it—on whether you and I live our lives as God wants." This is followed by a point lifted from a 1932 Intimate Notes entry likening souls to blocks of stone and God to the stonecutter. "Let us not try to draw aside," he writes, for if we do: "Instead of polished stone suitable for building, we will be a shapeless mass of gravel that people will trample on contemptuously" (no. 756).

One of the insights of the Christian tradition that the Second Vatican Council recaptured for the benefit of today's Catholics concerns the realization that the right and duty to participate in the mission of the Church—the "apostolate"—belong to everyone in the Church by virtue of Baptism and Confirmation. This also was a part of Escrivá's foundational insight in the 1930s, decades before Vatican II.

A key part of the apostolate of the laity, expressed in the title of the next chapter, is Winning New Apostles (nos. 790–812)—that is, opening the eyes of other Christians to their calling. One of the points here recalls a scene repeated more than once in Burgos in 1938 and 1939, as Escrivá strolled along the banks of the Arlanzon River, near the Sabadell Hotel, with some young soldier on leave who'd sought him out in order to open his heart to him. "Do you remember?" he writes. "Night was falling as you and I began our prayer. From close by came the murmur of water. And through the stillness of the Castilian city, we also seemed to hear voices of people from many lands, crying to us in anguish that they do not yet know Christ. Unashamedly you kissed your crucifix and you asked him to make you an apostle of apostles" (no. 811).

Next comes another of the author's favorite subjects—Little Things (nos. 813–830). So important to the quest for sanctity does he consider it that he writes: "'Great' holiness consists in carrying out the 'little' duties of each moment" (no. 817). Escrivá spelled that out further in a March 1937 letter to Jimenez Vargas, now part of no. 826 in *The Way*: "Everything we poor humans try to achieve—even sanctity—is a weave of little things which . . . can form an astonishing tapestry of heroism or villainy, of virtues or sins."

Attention to everyday things is a central element of the universal call to holiness as he understood it. Escrivá biographer Andres Vazquez de Prada remarks that this way of approaching life "places holiness . . . within arm's reach." But it doesn't imply an individualistic view of spirituality. The social implications of the little things are underlined in a point taken from a Honduran consulate meditation of June 19, 1937. Speaking of the bad things likely to happen when a little bolt comes loose in a big piece of machinery—"The whole work is slowed up. Perhaps the whole machine will be rendered useless"—Escrivá comments: "What a big thing it is to be a little bolt!" (no. 830).

After a chapter on Tactics (nos. 831–851) devoted to practical implications of a spirituality of little things, *The Way* turns naturally to Spiritual Childhood (nos. 852–874) and Life of Childhood (nos. 875–901). Here the influence of St. Thérèse of Lisieux is obvious. St. Thérèse (1873–1897), a Carmelite nun and mystic whom Pope John Paul II in 1997 designated a doctor of the Church, is one of the most popular and influential saints of modern times. Since her autobiography, *The Story of a Soul*, first appeared in 1898, it has sold millions of copies in many languages.

Spiritual childhood and the "little way" associated with it are central to her spirituality. In a typical passage

St. Thérèse writes: "Jesus has shown me the only path which leads to this divine furnace of love. It is the complete abandonment of a baby sleeping without fear in its father's arms. . . . Jesus does not demand great deeds. All He wants is self-surrender and gratitude. . . . He needs nothing from us except our love."

Escrivá's views on spiritual childhood reflect both the thinking of Thérèse of Lisieux and his own experience of God as summed up in the expression "divine filiation"—the awareness that we are God's adopted daughters and sons. Theologian Scott Hahn calls this sense of divine filiation the "foundation" of Opus Dei and "the source of freedom, confidence, purpose, ardor, and joy for all Christians who live and labor."

An incident that Escrivá turned into no. 897 of *The Way* was crucial in this regard. As recorded in his notebook on October 16, 1931, he was riding a streetcar in Madrid when: "I felt the action of the Lord. He was making spring forth in my heart and on my lips, with the force of something imperatively necessary, this tender invocation: *Abba! Pater!* I was out on the street, in a streetcar. . . . Probably I made that prayer out loud. And I walked the streets of Madrid for maybe an hour, maybe two, I can't say; time passed without my being aware of it. They must have thought I was crazy."

In speaking of the life of childhood, St. Josemaría expresses the attitude of a loving child toward his father—as, for instance, in no. 882: "Don't you see how I do everything wrong? Well, if you don't help me very much, I'll do it all even worse!" This comes from his Intimate Notes written October 2, 1931: "I will do your will. I want to do it. If I don't do it, it's because . . . you're not helping me." A hostile critic might see this as more childish than childlike; but these are the reflections of a mature man accustomed to working himself to the bone on behalf of a great cause: "Work tires you physically and leaves you unable to pray. But you're always in the presence of your Father. If you can't speak to him, look at him every now and then like a little child . . . and he'll smile at you" (no. 895). The words are from his Intimate Notes of June 1933.

Section Two: Vocation and Apostolic Mission (chapters 43–46)

Father Josemaría had a strong sense of vocation—his own vocation, the vocation to Opus Dei, the Christian vocation in general, the vocations of Catholic lay people. (We shall see more about this in the next chapter, where Escrivá's originality is discussed.) In *The Way* he regularly uses the word "calling" to express the idea, and Calling therefore is the title of chapter 43, on vocation (nos. 902–928).

"Why don't you give yourself to God once and for all . . . really . . . *now!*" he demands (no. 902). Pushy? But, as Vazquez de Prada points out, the question was one that Escrivá frequently put to himself. No. 905 uses the atmosphere of wartime Burgos to illuminate the real significance of vocation: "Patriotic fervor—which is praiseworthy—leads many men to give their lives in service, even in a 'crusade.' Don't forget that Christ, too, has 'crusaders' and people chosen for this service."

At the heart of any authentic spiritual calling is a powerful impetus to apostolate. By now *The Way* plainly is speaking to committed, well-formed Christians with a sense of their vocation, and so we get chapter 44, The Apostle (nos. 929–959), and its companion, chapter 45, The Apostolate (nos. 960–982). No. 933 expresses the fundamental idea of both: "There is a story of a soul who, on saying to our Lord in prayer, 'Jesus, I love you,' heard this reply from Heaven: 'Deeds are love—not sweet words.' Think if you also could deserve this gentle reproach." The anonymous "soul" was the author. The incident took place on February 16, 1932, shortly after he'd given communion to the sisters of the Foundation for the Sick. As he heard the words now repeated in *The Way*, he later wrote, "I saw clearly how little generosity I have. . . . O Jesus, help me, so that your donkey will be fully generous. Deeds, deeds!"

Apostolate takes many forms. Several are suggested here—for example, the "letter-writing apostolate," which is mentioned in nos. 976 and 977: "When I begin, I tell my guardian angel that all I hope from my letter is that it may do some good." Escrivá was a dedicated practitioner of this particular apostolate, as attested by *The Way* itself, which contains a substantial amount of material from letters he wrote and received.

The inclined plane comes to its end with—what else?—a chapter called Perseverance (nos. 983–999). The lesson is simple but absolutely necessary: "To begin is for everyone, to persevere is for saints" (no. 983).

Father Josemaría liked donkeys and often compared himself to one because, along with their other qualities, they are persevering beasts. Fittingly, therefore, a donkey is immortalized at the conclusion of the book. On July 18, 1938, he and several companions set out on a pilgrimage to the shrine of Santiago de Compostela, but they missed their train. A priest who was part of the little group called a cab, and soon they were riding twenty miles cross-country to catch up with the train, with Escrivá giving a meditation while they traveled. As they drove through the valley of Orbigo that bright summer day, they spied a donkey at a waterwheel, and on the spot the patient animal became part of Escrivá's meditation—and eventually of *The Way*, where the reader is invited to learn from his good example:

> O blessed perseverance of the donkey that turns the waterwheel! Always the same pace. Always around the same circle. One day after another, every day the same.
>
> Without that, there would be no ripeness in the fruit, nor blossom in the orchard, nor scent of flowers in the garden.
>
> Carry this thought to your interior life (no. 998).

People aren't donkeys, though, and their reason for persevering in the interior life—supposing they do—is radically different. *The Way*'s final point, no. 999, leaves no doubt what it is: "Love. Fall in Love, and you will not leave him."

⚜

An official document prepared as part of the process of beatification of St. Josemaría in 1992 (he was canonized—formally recognized as a saint—by Pope John Paul II ten years later, on October 6, 2002) contains this statement: "One can see that [Escrivá's] writings have preceded and anticipated the most important decisions of Vatican II. They have presented the ideal of ordinary Christian life in direct and fruitful contact with the gospel, which up to now had never appeared in the history of the Church."

That is a splendid tribute. But it can't compare with the silent tribute paid *The Way* by the ordinary people who turn to it regularly for guidance as they swagger, stagger, stride, and mince their respective ways up the inclined plane. In the homily quoted above, St. Josemaría remarks: "Today, as yesterday, heroism is expected of the Christian. A heroism in great struggles, if the need arises. Normally, however, heroism in the little skirmishes of each day." There, and only seldom anywhere else, is where sanctity lies for most people.

CHAPTER FIVE

THE ORIGINALITY OF ST. JOSEMARÍA ESCRIVÁ

Students of the thought of St. Josemaría Escrivá often speak of the originality of his vision as it's expressed in Opus Dei. Escrivá, however, declined to take credit for that. Opus Dei was God's work, not his, he insisted; he hadn't founded anything, and all he'd done was get in the way now and then.

Leaving aside that bit of modesty, there's probably truth in this analysis. After all, its members and friends are convinced, Opus Dei really is God's work. Still, we're entitled to suppose that, along with the divine inventiveness, some creativity of Escrivá's also is present in this ground-breaking group. John Allen calls the idea embodied in Opus Dei an "explosive concept, with the potential for unleashing Christian energy in many areas of endeavor." It seems likely that both God and St. Josemaría had a hand in that.

Granting, then, that it's reasonable to speak of Escrivá's creativity as a founder, it nonetheless would be a mistake to suppose that everything new and important about the group he founded was entirely original with him. On the contrary. Time and again, his most striking innovations had precedents.

Holiness as a realistic goal for lay people living and working in the world? St. Francis de Sales argued for that in the seventeenth century. The apostolate of the laity? St. Vincent Pallotti (1795–1850) promoted this idea in the nineteenth century, and Pope Pius XI, who occupied the chair of Peter from 1922 to 1939, sometimes was called "the Pope of Catholic Action" in recognition of his efforts on its behalf. The key place of spiritual childhood in the interior life? As we saw in the last chapter, this was a fundamental part of the teaching of St. Thérèse of Lisieux (1873–1897). In short, it's no exaggeration to say of many of St. Josemaría's most important foundational innovations: other people got there first.

So how can these things correctly be called innovations of his?

There are two answers to that. The first is that Escrivá usually didn't just take other people's good ideas and fit them into the Opus Dei framework. He reshaped the ideas, developed them, and thus created something distinctive and new. The second answer is precisely that "something new" itself: in other words, Opus Dei. Escrivá's ideas about the apostolate of the laity and sanctity for ordinary Christians in the world illustrate both of these points.

Apostolate and Sanctity

Back when Opus Dei was getting started—the 1920s and 1930s, that is—the dominant model of apostolate for lay members of the Catholic Church was Catholic Action. This movement was (and in some places even today, still is) an important, dynamic force in the Church, a channel of lay energy and commitment strongly encouraged by popes and bishops. Yet there also was a significant, built-in limitation in Catholic Action's rationale and self-understanding. The apostolate of the laity—their participation in the mission of the Church—was understood to be a form of participation in the apostolate of the clerical hierarchy. As such, what was done in the name of "Catholic Action" required approval, and ultimately control, by clerics—something that today is true of lay ministries and official programs carried out by lay people in the Church's name. In its day, Catholic Action represented a very positive step forward in involving lay people in ecclesial undertakings; in many places today, however, it would fall short of the urgent needs of both the Church and the world.

Escrivá proposed a different model, one resembling the Christian community in the earliest days of the Church. This model is based on the fact that the duty and right of lay people to take part in the redemptive mission of the Church—which itself continues the redemptive mission of Christ—come to them directly from him in the sacraments of baptism and confirmation. As far back as 1932 Father Josemaría wrote: "The prejudice that ordinary members of the faithful must limit themselves to helping the clergy in ecclesiastical apostolates has to be rejected. There is no reason why the secular apostolate should always be a mere participation in the apostolate of the hierarchy. Secular people too have a duty to do apostolate. Not because they receive a canonical mission, but because they are part of the Church. Their mission . . . is fulfilled in their profession, their job, their family, and among their colleagues and friends."

Three decades later the Second Vatican Council took the same approach in its Dogmatic Constitution on the Church, *Lumen Gentium*, as well as in its Decree on the Apostolate of Lay People, *Apostolicam Actuositatem*: "The apostolate of the laity is a sharing in the salvific mission of the Church. Through Baptism and Confirmation all are appointed to this apostolate by the Lord himself" (*Lumen Gentium*, 33). This is something St. Josemaría had been saying for thirty years.

Similarly—and difficult as it may be to imagine now—not so long ago the idea of sanctity for lay people, achieved in large part through their everyday work and the fulfillment of their ordinary duties, was also, practically speaking, something new in mainstream Catholic circles. To a great extent, that reflected the traditional idea of *contemptus mundi*—contempt for the world—that for so long shaped thinking about spirituality and the interior life, not only among Catholics but among other Christians as well.

As he was moving in the direction of becoming a Catholic, Scott Hahn recalls, "Opus Dei's sense of secularity touched me in a rather personal way. Coming from a Calvinist background, I had been taught to view the world and the fallen human race in terms of 'total depravity.'" In Opus Dei, Hahn encountered something radically different: Christian optimism and appreciation for the world, "an optimism founded on secularity—and on the biblical account of God's sovereignty over creation." This is the attitude summed up in memorable fashion in the title of a famous 1967 sermon by Escrivá: *Passionately Loving the World*.

But, someone might object, it's fundamentally unrealistic, a case of apples and oranges, to try to join a vigorous, traditional version of the interior life grounded in eschatological hope to active engagement in secular affairs, as Escrivá does. Nevertheless, as Father Richard John Neuhaus remarks (in his last, posthumously published book, *American Babylon*), "we should at least entertain the possibility . . . that other-worldly hope can intensify one's engagement in the responsibilities for this world." Indeed, Neuhaus adds, it's just in this way that "the present is given new urgency, raised to a new level of intensity, because it is riddled through and through with what is to be."

As John Allen observes, Opus Dei not uncommonly is viewed as a "traditional" alternative to "liberal" forms of Catholicism that emerged after Vatican II. Allen sees it somewhat differently: "[F]rom a historical point of view Opus Dei is not traditional at all. Its vision of laity and priests, women and men, sharing the same vocation and being part of the same body, all free to pursue that vocation within their professional sphere as they see fit, was so innovative that Escrivá was accused of heresy in 1940s Spain." It's said that when he first went to Rome, a Vatican official told him, "You've come a hundred years too soon."

Two of Escrivá's key ideas, unity of life and vocation, illustrate his originality and innovativeness. Points from *The Way* serve to illustrate them.

Unity of Life

There's a powerful and disturbing example of *dis*unity of life in a famous sequence in one of the Godfather movies. The child of a gang member is being baptized in a Catholic church; at the same time, other gang members are engaged in a series of execution-style killings around town. The director cuts back and forth between the two things—religious ritual, murder and mayhem—to create a chilling effect. As the sequence unfolds, viewers are likely to think—though probably not in just these words—"Some of these people don't have a whole lot of unity of life."

Gangland killings side-by-side with a baptism represent an extreme case, but everyday disunity of life is all too common. The Second Vatican Council made that point in its pastoral constitution on the Church in the Modern World: "One of the gravest errors of our time is the dichotomy between the faith which many profess and the practice of their daily lives.... Let there... be no such pernicious opposition between professional and social activity on the one hand and religious life on the other.... It is their task [i.e., the task of the Catholic laity] to cultivate a properly informed conscience and to impress the divine law on the affairs of the earthly city" (*Gaudium et Spes*, no. 43). Reading that, you'd almost suppose the council looked ahead a few years and saw on the horizon the scandal of pro-choice Catholic politicians who declare themselves personally opposed to abortion while supporting laws that permit and even encourage it.

Years earlier, St. Josemaría was sensitive to this problem as he then found it, and he spoke of it in *The Way*: "Have you ever bothered to think how absurd it is to leave one's Catholicism aside on entering a university, or a professional association, or a scholarly meeting, or Congress, as if you were checking your hat at the door?" (no. 353). And again: "Faith. It's a pity to see how frequently many Christians have it on their lips and yet how sparingly they put it into their actions. You would think it a virtue to be preached only, and not one to be practiced" (no. 579). And in one of the book's most sharply worded passages he skewers the hypocrisy of the halfhearted:

> I see you, Christian gentleman (that's what you say you are), kissing an image, muttering some vocal prayer, crying out against those who attack the Church of God, even frequenting the holy sacraments.

But I don't see you making a sacrifice, nor avoiding certain conversations of a worldly nature (I could with justice have used another adjective!), nor being generous toward those in need (including that same Church of God!), nor putting up with a failing in one of your brothers, nor checking your pride for the sake of the common good, nor getting rid of that tight cloak of selfishness, nor . . . so many other things!

Yes, I see you. . . . But I don't see you. . . . And yet, you say you are a Christian gentleman! What a poor idea you have of Christ! (no. 683).

So what does unity of life look like?

Pope John Paul II was a remarkable example of it. Pope Wojtyla radiated an aura of wholeness and integrity—qualities of someone who knew who he was and where he was going, and had shaped the multiple elements of his life and personality into a consistent, coherent set of values and pattern of behavior that expressed his sense of self-identity and purpose.

St. Paul is another instance, and a very interesting one. After his conversion, he too projected this wholeness and integrity, reached by essentially the same means—deep, interior identification with Jesus: "I have been crucified with Christ; it is no longer I who live, but Christ who lives in me; and the life I now live in the flesh I live by faith in the Son of God" (Galatians 2:20). At the same time, though, he's also a conflicted man: "For I do not do the good I want, but the evil I do not want is what I do" (Romans 7:19). But if Paul truly identifies with Christ, how can that be?

The answer is that unity of life apparently involved an ongoing struggle on Paul's part. (Perhaps, for all the rest of us know, it also required that on the part of John Paul II.) It may very well have remained a work in progress to the end. There's consolation here for us weak Christians, who know how inconsistent and feeble our own efforts to achieve and practice this holy integration of the self really are.

Unity of life means far, far more than being consistent, well organized, systematic. These are excellent things, but true unity of life goes much further and deeper, reaching buried recesses of our personalities and our lives—emotions and impulses of which much of the time we are barely conscious, fleeting (but recurring and troubling) thoughts, relationships tinged by negativity that we prefer not to acknowledge—and bringing healing to them. While the effort it requires of us is very great, in the end it isn't something we can accomplish for ourselves. It is the result of God's grace at work in us, overcoming the effects of sin. Our cooperation is essential; but finally it is grace that produces this kind of unity.

Point no. 2 in *The Way* gives simple, powerful testimony to the fundamental idea: "May your behavior and your conversation be such that everyone who sees or hears you can say: This man reads the life of Jesus Christ." The key to unity of life for Christians lies in being persons who struggle to model their lives on Christ's and, with the help of grace, truly become other Christs of whom it can in a real sense be said that Christ lives in them.

St. Josemaría speaks of that struggle in these words:

> Purity of intention. The suggestions of pride and the impulses of the flesh are not difficult to recognize.... And you fight, and with grace, you conquer.
>
> But the motives that inspire you, even in your holiest actions, don't seem clear. And deep down inside you hear a voice which makes you aware of your human motives . . . so

that your soul is subtly haunted by the disturbing thought that you are not acting as you should—for pure love, solely and exclusively to give God all his glory.

React at once each time and say: "Lord, for myself I want nothing. All for your glory and for love" (*The Way*, no. 788).

About Commitment

Two principles lie at the heart of the struggle to achieve unity of life: commitment and vocation.

Commitment in this context doesn't have its ordinary meaning—a promise or pledge to do or be something or other, including doing something as simple as showing up on time for an appointment or remembering to return a borrowed book. It refers instead to a particular kind of choice—a very large choice, you might say, which is both starting point and framework for the many implementing choices that will be needed to carry it out. The choice by a man and a woman to marry each other is a commitment in this sense; here is a choice that will demand innumerable implementing choices (and corresponding acts) to live it out, right up to the time one party or the other dies. The choice of a careeer, the choice of a way of life such as the clerical state or the state of consecrated life are other examples.

One of the noteworthy things about a commitment is that it's open-ended. At no point, for instance, can a man say he's done everything required by a commitment to be someone else's friend and doesn't need to do anything else—the friendship is now complete. On the contrary, for as long as the friendship lasts, there will always be more to do in order to keep it alive and healthy; and if by chance someone does begin to act as if nothing more were required to express and live out this friendship, it's a good bet that the friendship will soon begin to wither and die. At the start, though, there's no telling just what this "more" will turn out to be. Only the living out of the friendship over time can reveal that. This is true of any commitment: only time and experience can make clear all that it will require in practical, concrete terms, even though some things incompatible with the commitment will be obvious from the start (infidelity in marriage, for instance).

All this also is true of the commitment of faith—essentially, a commitment to friendship with a person, Jesus Christ—which is the fundamental commitment of Christian life. St. Josemaría had a lively awareness of the centrality of this commitment in creating and sustaining unity of life. "The cross on your breast? Good. But the cross on your shoulders, the cross in your flesh, the cross in your mind. Thus will you live for Christ, with Christ, and in Christ; only thus will you be an apostle" (*The Way*, no. 929).

Often, making and keeping commitments isn't easy. Whether to be a physician or to be a priest, to marry this person or that one—these are serious and sometimes difficult questions calling for a high degree of self-knowledge as well as a clear-eyed grasp of present realities and future probabilities: the virtue of prudence, in other words. Trustworthy advice and counsel ("direction") are highly desirable.

And when the questions have been answered and the commitment has been made, the hard work of living it out has probably just begun. Problems are almost certain to arise along the way. For instance: how to handle a conflict between or among one's commitments, such as the conflicting demands of work and family life. Ideally, people in conflict situations will consult their personal vocations and resolve the conflict in light of them. But that is not so easy for someone who's never given much thought to vocation and has no clear notion what his or her personal vocation might actually be.

About Vocation

We saw above that the idea of vocation—"calling" was the word he typically used—holds an important position in St. Josemaría's thought. "Don't doubt it: your vocation is the greatest grace our Lord could have given you. Thank him for it," he wrote (*The Way*, no. 913). Very likely he meant especially the vocation to membership in Opus Dei. But since *The Way* is written not just for members of Opus Dei but for anyone serious about the interior life, what's said about vocation has universal application.

In this regard, St. Josemaría's strong feelings on the subject of clericalism are especially relevant. The word clericalism often is used to refer to inappropriate intervention by clerics in politics, something that in certain times and places has been a serious problem. Escrivá, however, understood clericalism in a more comprehensive sense of which the political aspect is only one part, and he deplored the harm it causes.

He wasn't alone in that. Someone once asked Flannery O'Connor why she, a Catholic, wrote stories about Bible Belt Protestants. This was her answer:

> To a lot of Protestants I know, monks and nuns are fanatics, none greater. And to a lot of the monks and nuns I know, my Protestant prophets are fanatics. For my part, I think the only difference between them is that if you are a Catholic and have this intensity of belief you join the

convent and are heard from no more; whereas if you are a Protestant and have it, there is no convent for you to join and you go about in the world, getting into all sorts of trouble and drawing the wrath of people who don't believe anything at all down on your head."

The founder of Opus Dei probably would have appreciated that. O'Connor is describing and subtly skewering a fundamental assumption of the clericalist mentality: "If you are a Catholic and have... intensity of belief you join the convent"—i.e., enter religious life or the priesthood. This was how many Catholics thought in her day, and it remains how many think now. It doesn't offer much encouragement to Catholics like Flannery O'Connor, whose belief also is intense but who are aware that God hasn't called them to the consecrated life or the clerical state.

"I find clericalism repellent and I understand how, as well as an evil anticlericalism, there also exists a healthy anticlericalism," Escrivá said. Since the clericalist mentality—which currently is probably shared by at least as many lay people as clerics—originates in confusion about the nature of vocation, overcoming it requires understanding and accepting the fact that not just clerics and religious but lay people as well have vocations, and that every baptized person has a unique personal vocation of his or her own.

The theme of personal vocation occurs often in the writing of John Paul II. Its importance is especially clear in *Christifideles Laici*, his 1988 document on the laity. John Paul speaks here in a number of places about personal vocation; in a key passage he writes:

> The fundamental objective of the formation of the lay faithful is an ever-clearer discovery of one's vocation and

the ever-greater willingness to live it so as to fulfill one's mission.... This personal vocation and mission defines the dignity and the responsibility of each member of the lay faithful and makes up the focal point of the whole work of formation.... In fact, from eternity God has thought of us and has loved us as unique individuals. Every one of us he called by name.... Only in the unfolding of the history of our lives and its events is the eternal plan of God revealed to each of us. Therefore, it is a gradual process; in a certain sense, one that happens day by day (*Christifideles Laici*, no. 58).

St. Josemaría saw that and saw as well the special place in the spiritual struggle occupied by perseverance in one's own vocation:

Do you hear these words? "In another state in life, in another place, in another another position or occupation, you would do much more good." Talent isn't needed for what you are doing." Well, listen to me: Wherever you have been placed, you please God . . . and what you've just been thinking is clearly a suggestion of the devil" (*The Way*, no. 709). And again: "How anxious people are to get out of place! Think of what would happen if each bone and each muscle of the human body wanted to occupy some position other than its own. There is no other reason for the world's discontent. Continue where you are, my son; right where you are . . . how much you'll be able to work for the true kingdom of our Lord! (*The Way*, no. 832).

Especially Escrivá understood how the vocations of individual lay people serve to specify and make concrete the baptismal vocation common to all Christians. In an interview in 1968 he said:

I have always thought that the basic characteristic of the development of the laity is a new awareness of the dignity of the Christian vocation. God's call, the character conferred by Baptism, and grace mean that every single Christian can and should be a living expression of the faith. Every Christian should be "another Christ," "Christ himself," present among men.... This brings with it a deeper awareness of the Church as a community made up of all the faithful, where all share in one and the same mission, which each should fulfill according to his personal circumstances.

Vocation understood like this has a number of characteristics.

It is apostolic and evangelistic. *"Et regni eius non erit finis*—'His kingdom will have no end.' Doesn't it fill you with joy to work for a kingdom like that?" (*The Way*, no. 906).

While it is proper to the individual, it's typically lived out in company with others. "Your ideal, your vocation: it's madness. And your friends, your brothers: they're crazy. Haven't you heard that cry deep down within you sometimes? Answer firmly that you are grateful to God for the honor of being one of those 'lunatics'" (*The Way*, no. 910).

It is an aspect of divine filiation. "By calling you to be an apostle, our Lord has reminded you, so that you will never forget it, that you are a child of God" (*The Way*, no. 919).

It requires that one have an active interior life in order to persevere. "Pray always for perseverance for yourself and for your companions in the apostolate. Our adversary, the devil, knows only too well that you are his great enemies... and when he sees a fall in your ranks, how pleased he is!" (*The Way*, no. 924).

In view of St. Josemaría's concern for the subject of vocation, however, some people may consider it strange that *The Way* contains no specific treatment of vocational discernment—the more or less structured process by which someone comes to see and accept God's will in a serious, life-orienting matter requiring a choice: e.g., state in life, profession, marriage partner. It's possible of course that he simply overlooked it. More likely, though, he didn't see any special need to spell out a particular process or procedure for learning God's will, since someone striving for a constant sense of the presence of God, open to what God wants in every circumstance, faithful to the teaching and law of the Church, and enjoying the help of a reliable spiritual director—things repeatedly emphasized in *The Way*—is entitled to suppose that God will show him or her what he wants in his own good time. (Similarly, *The Way* contains no special instructions about methods of prayer. As we saw earlier, Escrivá's advice to someone who wants to start praying amounts to: Start. God, he believed, could be trusted to lend a hand after that.)

Every Christian has his or her unique, unrepeatable part in the plan of God. Of each of us it can be said that "we are [God's] workmanship, created in Christ Jesus for good works, which God prepared beforehand, that we should walk in them" (Eph. 2:10). With or without the help of a formal discernment process, it's imperative that we see, accept, and live out our particular roles in the great drama of redemption, unfolding our personal vocations step by step as we do:

> You are right. "The peak," you write me, "dominates the country for miles around, and yet there is not a single

plain to be seen: just one mountain after another. At times the landscape seems to level out, but then the mist rises and reveals another range that had been hidden." So it is, so it must be, with the horizon of your apostolate: the world has to be crossed. But there are no roads made for you. You yourselves will make the way through the mountains, beating it out by your own footsteps (*The Way*, no. 928).

This is how it is for Christians collectively, as members of the Church. It is also the challenge of living out his or her personal vocation facing each of us as we climb the inclined plane of friendship with God.

"We cannot have a split personality if we want to be Christians," Escrivá said. "There is only one life, made of flesh and spirit. And it is that life which has to become, in both body and soul, holy and filled with God." The idea isn't new. But his single-minded perseverance in pursuing it for himself and seeking to share it with others puts it at the heart of the originality of St. Josemaría Escrivá.

Acknowledgment and Sources

I wish to extend special thanks to Ismael Virto. Not only did the idea for this book originate with him but he also translated significant portions of Pedro Rodriguez's monumental critical-historical edition of *Camino* to assist me in my research and offered valuable advice and encouragement throughout the process of researching and writing. The book would not exist without him—although its failings and defects obviously are my responsibility, not his.

Besides *The Way*, I made use of the following by St. Josemaría Escrivá: *Conversations with Saint Josemaría Escrivá*, which also includes the important homily "Passionately Loving the World" (New York: Scepter Publishers, 2007); *Growing on the Inside: Notes from the Preaching of the Founder of Opus Dei, Madrid 1937* (Rome: privately printed, 2001); and "Interior Struggle" in *Christ Is Passing By* (Manila: Sinag-Tala Publishers, 1977; also published by Scepter).

Other works consulted include: John L. Allen, Jr., *Opus Dei: An Objective Look Behind the Myths and Reality of the Most Controversial Force in the Catholic Church* (New York: Doubleday, 2005); Michael Burleigh, *Sacred Causes: The Clash of Religion and Politics from the Great War to the War on Terror* (New York: HarperCollins, 2007); John Coverdale, *Uncommon Faith: The Early Years of Opus Dei*

(1928–1943) (New York: Scepter, 2002); G. Derville, *Une connaissance d'amour. Note de théologie sur l'edition critico-historique de Chemin (I, II)*, in *Studia et documenta*, 1 (2007), pp. 191–220; 3 (2007), pp. 277–305; Most Rev. Javier Echevarria, "Introduction" in *The Way* (New York: Doubleday Image Books, 2006); Francois Gondrand, *At God's Pace* (London and New York: Scepter, 1989); Scott Hahn, *Ordinary Work, Extraordinary Grace* (New York: Doubleday, 2006); Pope John Paul II, *Christifideles Laici*, On the Vocation and the Mission of the Lay Faithful in the Church and in the World; Vittorio Messori, *Opus Dei: Leadership and Vision in Today's Catholic Church* (Washington, D.C.: Regnery, 1997); Richard John Neuhaus, *American Babylon: Notes of a Christian Exile* (New York: Basic Books, 2009); George Orwell, *Homage to Catalonia* (Boston: Beacon Press, 1952); Pedro Rodriguez, ed., *Camino: Edicion Critico-Historica* (Madrid: Ediciones Rialp S.A., 2002); Pedro Rodriguez, Fernando Ocariz, Jose Luis Illanes, *Opus Dei in the Church: A Theological Reflection on the Spirit and Apostolate of Opus Dei* (New York: Scepter, 2003); St. Thérèse of Lisieux, *The Autobiography of St. Thérèse of Lisieux: The Story of a Soul* (Garden City, N.Y.: Doubleday Image Books, 1957); Hugh Thomas, *The Spanish Civil War* (New York: Modern Library, 1989); Vatican Council II, *Lumen Gentium*, Dogmatic Constitution on the Church, *Gaudium et Spes*, Pastoral Constitution on the Church in the Modern World, and *Apostolicam Actuositatem*, Decree on the Apostolate of Lay People; and Andres Vazquez de Prada, *The Founder of Opus Dei: The Life of Josemaría Escrivá*, Volume I, *The Early Years* (Princeton, N.J.: Scepter, 2001), and Volume II, *God and Daring* (New York: Scepter, 2003).